SOCRATES AND OTHER SAINTS

KALOS

The word *kalos* (καλός) means beautiful. It is the call of the good; that which arouses interest, desire: "I am here." Beauty brings the appetite to rest at the same time as it wakens the mind from its daily slumber, calling us to look afresh at that which is before our very eyes. It makes virgins of us all, and of everything—there, before us, lies something that we never noticed before. Beauty consists in *integritas sive perfectio* [integrity and perfection] and *claritas* [brightness/clarity]. It is the reason why we rise and why we sleep—that great night of dependence, one that reveals the borrowed existence of all things, if, that is, there is to be a thing at all, or if there is to be a person at all. Here lies the ground of all science, of philosophy, and of all theology, indeed of our each and every day.

This series will seek to provide intelligent-yet-accessible volumes that have the innocence of beauty and of true adventure, and in so doing remind us all again of that which we took for granted, most of all thought itself.

SERIES EDITORS:

Conor Cunningham, Eric Austin Lee, and Christopher Ben Simpson

Socrates and Other Saints

EARLY CHRISTIAN UNDERSTANDINGS OF REASON AND PHILOSOPHY

Dariusz Karłowicz

Translated by Artur Sebastian Rosman
With a foreword by Rémi Brague

CASCADE *Books* · Eugene, Oregon

SOCRATES AND OTHER SAINTS
Early Christian Understandings of Reason and Philosophy

Cascade Books
An Imprint of Wipf and Stock Publishers
199 W. 8th Ave., Suite 3
Eugene, OR 97401

www.wipfandstock.com

PAPERBACK ISBN: 978-1-4982-7873-7
HARDCOVER ISBN: 978-1-4982-7875-1
EBOOK ISBN: 978-1-4982-7874-4

Cataloguing-in-Publication data:

Names: Karłowicz, Dariusz, 1964–. | Rosman, Artur Sebastian

Title: Socrates and other saints : early Christian understandings of reason and philosophy / Dariusz Karłowicz, with a foreword by Rémi Brague

Description: Eugene, OR: Cascade Books, 2016 | Series: Kalos # | Includes bibliographical references and index.

Identifiers: ISBN 978-1-4982-7873-7 (paperback) | ISBN 978-1-4982-7875-1 (hardcover) | ISBN 978-1-4982-7874-4 (ebook)

Subjects: LCSH: Hellenism | Philosophy, Ancient | Fathers of the church | Faith and reason

Classification: BR128.8 K37 2017 (print) | BR128.8 (ebook)

Manufactured in the U.S.A.   JANUARY 24, 2017

Originally published in Polish in 2005 as *Sokrates i inni święci* © Fronda Pl. Sp. Z 0.0

For Juliusz Domański with gratitude

Table of Contents

Foreword

THE CHURCH FATHERS NEVER were totally forgotten. But, more often than not, they were read with a teleological optics. Controversial theology, beginning in the sixteenth century, looked for forerunners of Catholic or Reformed dogmatics, but made high standards of philological and historical accuracy necessary.[1] Neo-Scholasticism saw them as paving the way for more elaborate theological syntheses, in particular the work of Thomas Aquinas. Their works were excerpted and used as arguments, but seldom studied for their own sake.

An impressive witness of the interest of the nineteenth century for patristics, as well as a moving evidence for the high cultural level of the French clergy in the said period, is the mighty enterprise of a Catholic priest, Jacques-Paul Migne (d. 1875). His methods in dealing with former editors were seldom on the right side of the copyright laws, as the amusing biography that R. Howard Bloch devoted to him shows.[2] Yet, the result is there, an impressive monument of more than four-hundred in-quarto volumes, so widely known and taken advantage of that new editions of patristic texts always refer in their margins to the columns of Migne's *Patrologia Graeca* and *Patrologia Latina*, even if their level of scholarly accuracy is way above that of Migne's volumes.

Special mention must be made of fathers Claude Mondésert and Henri de Lubac, both were Jesuits, and of the series *Sources Chrétiennes*, founded in the darkest hours of the Second World War (1942), and in the wake of which many collections were produced in several languages.

Yet, the philosophers who paid attention to the writings of the church fathers are not that many. To the best of my knowledge, there is still no equivalent of Hans Jonas' work on the gnostics, i.e., of an interpretation of religious thinkers by means of conceptual tools borrowed from philosophy. The nearest approach we possess is Harry A. Wolfson's huge first volume of a monograph

1. See the keen observation of Ch. Dawson, "Edward Gibbon and the Fall of Rome" [1934], v, in: *Dynamics of World History* (Wilmington: ISI Books, 2002), 353.

2. R. Howard Bloch, *God's Plagiarist: Being an Account of the Fabulous Industry and Illegal Commerce of the Abbé Migne* (Chicago: University of Chicago Press, 1995).

that never was completed,[3] although Wolfson's approach was more history of ideas than philosophy. A noteworthy exception is Hans Blumenberg (d. 1996), who frequently quoted Arnobius and Lactantius, authors who are often looked down upon by his colleagues. The German philosopher Theo Kobusch has recently come up with a book that defends a bold thesis: Christianity is the full coming-to-itself of Platonism, its "truth" in the Hegelian meaning of this phrase. Furthermore, it introduced onto the philosophical stage a new object: subjectivity.[4]

Augustine is the exception that confirms the rule. Not to mention more or less casual references to utterances by him in Husserl (on the "inner man" as place of the truth) and Wittgenstein (on the way children learn to speak), Heidegger devoted a whole lecture-course to the *Confessions*.[5] More recently, Jean-Luc Marion has proposed a challenging phenomenological interpretation of Augustine's approach to subjectivity.[6]

In the present book, Dariusz Karłowicz chose to write as a philosopher interested in the philosophical aspects of some church fathers. He limits his research to a definite period of time. Not the very earliest period: the so-called Apostolic Fathers (Ignatius, Clement of Rome) are left out of the picture. Rather, he focuses on Tertullian, Justin, Clement of Alexandria. The anonymous "Epistle to Diognetus" and Origen are mentioned only twice, the Cappadocians never. This period can be characterized on historical and philosophical grounds.

Historically, it antedates the turning-point of Constantine's "conversion" and of the Council of Nicea. Dariusz Karłowicz points out that the historical situation of the ante-Nicene fathers is very much the same as our own [9–10]. Whether this is a drawback or a chance is an open question. The Constantinian era may have been a parenthesis only on the backdrop of a "normal" situation of estrangement of Christianity vis-à-vis the surrounding culture. Not necessarily a persecution, although the last century has produced a number of martyrs that dwarf the victims of Nero or Diocletian. The present one might itself make it look like the botched performance of amateurs.

Philosophically, Dariusz Karłowicz chooses to focus on the crucial period of the first encounter of Christianity and philosophy. Hence, we are

---

3. H. A. Wolfson, *The Philosophy of the Church Fathers*, vol. 1: *Faith, Trinity, Incarnation* (Cambridge: Harvard University Press, 1956).

4. T. Kobusch, *Christliche Philosophie: Die Entdeckung der Subjektivität* (Darmstadt: Wissenschaftliche Buchgesellschaft, 2006).

5. M. Heidegger, *Augustinus und der Neuplatonismus* (Summer 1921), Gesamtausgabe, vol. 60, edited by C. Strube (Frankfurt: Klostermann, 1995).

6. J.-L. Marion, *Au lieu de soi: L'approche de saint Augustin* (Paris: P.U.F., 2008).

before the Cappadocians. With them, especially Gregory of Nyssa, Plato's influence becomes unmistakable, although Platonism never was swallowed with hook, line, and sinker, but always corrected and completed on essential points.[7] Not to mention later authors like Pseudo-Dionysius the Areopagite, who lived around 500, who heavily drew on Proclus, or Leontius of Byzantium and Maximus Confessor, both steeped in Aristotelian logic and metaphysics.

The very first Christian writers had few contacts with technical philosophy. This must be explained, in order to correct a fallacy arising from the very way in which we perceive the ancient world. For us, this world is present first and foremost thanks to its literary legacy. The ancient world means: ancient literature and art. Hence, we spontaneously think of the ancient mind as being ancient philosophy. But philosophy was in the ancient world the privilege of a rather narrow cultural elite. Philosophers did not write for the common run of mankind.[8] "Doing philosophy" was perceived as a means to escape from the vulgar.[9] Furthermore, we must distinguish inside "philosophy" itself. There were several levels in the offer of philosophical goods on the ancient market. There were high-brow schools, like the Neoplatonic one that combined an elementary initiation to logic, physics, and ethics, based on the textbooks of Aristotle, and a higher revelation contained in Plato's dialogues. This kind of philosophy was upheld by small circles of highly educated, and more often than not pretty affluent, teachers who were often related by blood. Underneath, there were popular philosophers who belonged to the Stoic or Epicurean tradition and preached for the lower classes. Those are the philosophers who got in touch with St. Paul (Acts 17:18) as well as with the rabbis of the Talmud. The latter coined the word אפיקורוס, "Epicurus," to designate the unbeliever, more precisely the people who deny the existence of God's providence.[10] The subtleties of "higher" philosophy were not directly known by the early church fathers, who had to put up with textbooks of doxography. Now, the bulk of what we call "ancient philosophy" is for us the library of the late, decidedly high-brow Neoplatonic schools, that comprised the works of the professors (Plotinus, Proclus, Damascius) and the "classical works" they commented upon, i.e., Plato and Aristotle.

In order to better understand the stance taken by the church fathers toward philosophy, it is apposite to enlarge our ken to the whole of Greek culture and to get rid of a received wisdom, the supposed Hellenization of early

7. E. von Ivánka, *Plato Christianus: Übernahme und Umgestaltung des Platonismus durch die Väter* (Einsiedeln: Johannes Verlag, 1964).

8. See, e.g., Porphyry, *De abstinentia*, I, 27, 28 & IV, 18, 7.

9. See, e.g., Lucian, *Hermotimus*, §§15, 21, 52, 67.

10. Mishnah, Sanhedrin, X, 1; Avot, II, 14.

Christianity. The very idea of a Hellenism superseding the supposedly purely Semitic preaching of Jesus or the primitive community, as Dariusz Karłowicz shows, has not a leg to stand on. There never was such a thing as pure "Hellenism" nor, for that matter, pure "Semitism." When Jesus preached, Palestine had been under Hellenistic rule for three centuries, and the eastern part of the Roman Empire was administrated in Greek rather than in Latin. The Greek word for "palanquin," *phoreion*, has found its way into the Hebrew Bible as *'appiryōn* (Song 3:9). The Hellenization took place among the Jewish communities of the Mediterranean seaports, and first of all in Alexandria, where the Septuagint translation gives evidence of the encounter. An encounter between Christianity and Greek *paideia* was hardly avoidable, nay it was normal.[11]

According to the usual picture, the fathers adopted towards Greek philosophy contrary attitudes. Some welcomed it by means of different strategies of appropriation, whereas some bluntly rejected its claims. Those attitudes are often symbolized by two heroes: Justin and Tertullian. Now, Dariusz Karłowicz shows that Tertullian does not attack reason as such and that Justin is not so staunch a rationalist as commonly admitted. For him, philosophy sees a part of the whole truth, but only a part of it [59].There never was a frontal opposition between Christianity and philosophy as two blocks. A great diversity obtained in both camps. The Christians were not only those whom we consider at present as orthodox, like the church fathers. People whom we consider now as "heretics" were in there, too. On the side of the philosophers, schools fought with each other. There never was a common front of philosophy against its opponents, at least before a relatively late date, when Porphyry inaugurated the tradition of the harmonies between Plato and Aristotle[12] that was to be taken up by Arabic philosophers like al-Fārābī (d. 950)[13] and lasted in Europe till the fifteenth century, the Italian *Quattrocento*. The watershed may have been Gemistos Plethon's polemics against Aristotle, which led to the grounding of the so-called Platonic Academy in Florence.

In earlier times, philosophers poked fun at each other and hardly pulled their punches. Stoics and Epicureans don't pamper each other in Cicero's dialogues. Plutarch launched broadsides against both schools. Now, the church

---

11. See Werner Jaeger, *Early Christianity and Greek Paideia.* There is a commodious bilingual edition English / Italian (Milan: Bompiani, 2013).

12. See the pathbreaking article by P. Hadot, «L'harmonie des philosophies de Platon et d'Aristote selon Porphyre dans le commentaire de Dexippe sur les Catégories» [1974], in: *Plotin, Porphyre. Etudes Néoplatoniciennes* (Paris: Les Belles Lettres, 1999), 335–82.

13. Al-Fārābī, *L'armonia delle opinioni dei due sapienti il divino Platone e Aristotele. Introduzione, testo arabo, traduzione e commento di Cecilia Martini Bonadeo* (Pisa: Plus, 2008).

fathers more often than not used the intellectual tools that had been handed over to them by the philosophers they criticized.

Dariusz Karłowicz is careful to do openly what many people recoil from doing, i.e., distinguishing the stance towards reason and the stance towards philosophy [35]. On the one hand, Christianity never was the enemy of reason. The phrase *sacrificium intellectus* is often misunderstood because of a faulty construction of the genitive, which is in this case subjective and, heaven forfend, not objective! The intellect is not what is sacrificed, but what sacrifices, not the victim, but the priest that offers God a "verbal cult," the *logikh latreia* of St. Paul (Rom 12:1). We are miles away from a praise of stupidity. Moreover, *pistis*, that we translate with "faith," is supposed by philosophers, too. Some trust is necessary for whoever wants to learn (*dei pisteuein ton manqanonta*):[14] trust in the truthfulness and sincerity of the teacher. More basically still, trust in the truthfulness of our intellectual tools.

But, on the other hand, philosophy doesn't possess any monopoly vis-à-vis rationality, nay it is not always the rightful heir of reason [69]. The basic concept that makes philosophy possible is nature (*physis*).[15] Now, even this basic concept is not always adequately dealt with by philosophers [75]. Somehow blinded by the dazzling light of their discovery, the first ones mistook the autonomy of nature's laws for self-position and made of nature some self-positing Being, to use Scholastic parlance an *ens a se*, almost a god.

Many centuries afterwards, Spinoza made the same kind of mistake when he defined his "substance" as what exists by itself without requiring any external factor.[16] This boils down to conflating two meanings of being, the existential and the predicative in its definitional use. A substance (*ousia*), in the original definition of this word of art of Aristotelian philosophy, is what does not require anything else in order to be what it is, i.e., to possess the "essential" properties that it must possess in order to *be* what it is. It doesn't mean that a substance should be able to *exist* by itself.

A more balanced view should acknowledge at least the possibility of a creation, together with the stable nature of created beings that enables them to become the object of scientific knowledge.[17]

---

14. Aristotle, *Sophistical Refutations*, 2, 165b3.

15. L. Strauss, *Natural Right and History* (Chicago: University of Chicago Press, 1953), 81–83.

16. Spinoza, *Ethica more geometrico demonstrata*, Definition 3, Proposition VII.

17. See Augustine, *De Genesi ad litteram*, IX, 17, ed. Zycha (Vienna: Tempsky, 1894), 291 (*naturales leges*); Thomas Aquinas, *Summa contra Gentiles*, III, 69 (Rome: Leonina, 1934), 304a (*cognitio scientiae naturalis*).

It might be the case that the real intellectual fight in Late Antiquity was fought not between dogmas, but between worldviews and the ways of life that they fostered in response to them. Hans Urs von Balthasar once observed, *en passant*, probably in the wake of Nietzsche, that the real adversary of Christian salvation is not Greek philosophy, but the vision of life and being that comes to the fore in Greek tragedy.[18] Very much in an analogous way, Dariusz Karłowicz points out that philosophy was, for pagans as well as for Christians, for its practitioners as well as for for its enemies, less a set of dogmas (although the word is philosophic in origin) as a way of life. He thereby takes advantage of the works of Pierre Hadot who highlighted this dimension of ancient philosophy.

Possibly, the same fight is still a living issue for us and has not lost anything of its pungency. The Socratic model of life of constant enquiry is very nice, but it precludes from the possibility that the Truth is given. One knows Lessing's parable in which the choice is between the Truth and the search for the Truth.[19] The German playwright and philologist contended that we human beings should choose enquiry over the Truth, for the latter is God's privilege. So far so good. But how could we know that we are really looking for truth and not for our own intellectual excitement. Furthermore, what if God had somehow *wanted* to present us with Truth?

Rémi Brague

18. H. U. von Balthasar, *Rechenschaft 1965* (Einsiedeln: Johannes Verlag, 1965), 24.

19. G. E. Lessing, *Eine Duplik, 1, end; Werke* t. 8 (Darmstadt: Wissenschaftliche Buchgesellschaft, 1996), 33.

Primary Source Abbreviations

All primary sources are quoted from Philip Schaff's (ed.) *Ante-Nicene Fathers* and *Nicene Post-Nicene Fathers* unless noted by asterisk (*).

Ad. Diog	*Ad Diognetum*
Aristides	[Aristid.]
Apol.	*Apologia*
Augustinus	
De vita beata	
De civ. Dei	*De civitate Dei*
De doctrina Christiana	
Cicero [Cic.]	
Ac.	*Academica (1=Posteriora, 2=Priora=Lucullus)*
Fin.	*De finibus bonorum et malorum*
Leg.	*De legibus*
Nat. deor.	*De natura deorum*
Off.	*De officiis*
Rep.	*De re publica*
Tusc.	*Tusculanae disputationes*
Clemens Alexandrinus [Clem. Al.]	
Str.	*Stromata*
Protr.	*Protrepticus*
Clemens Romanus [Clem. Rom.]	
Epist.	*Epistula Clementis*

Eusebius [Eus.]
HE   *Historia ecclesiae*

Hermias [Herm.]
Irr.   *Irrisio gentilium philosophorum*

Hieronymus [Hier.]
*Epist.   *Epistulae*

**Hippolitus [Hippol.]
*Ref.   *Refutatio omnium haeresium*

Irenaeus [Iren.]
Adv. haer.   *Adversus haereses*
Demonstr.   *Demonstratio apostolicae praedicationis*

Iustinus [Iust.]
Apol.   *Apologia*
Dial.   *Dialogus cum Tryphone Iudaeo*

Lucianus
*Herm.   *Hermotimus*
*Pisc.   *Piscator*

Minucius Felix [Min. Fel.]
Oct.   *Octavius*

Origenes
*Cels.   *Contra Celsum*

Philon Alexandrinus [Phil. Al.]
*Leg. alleg.   *Leges allegoriarum*
*De opif.   *De opificio mundi*

Plato [Pl.]
*R.   *Respublica*
*Tht.   *Theaetetus*

Plutarchus [Plut.]
Vitae parallelae
Cat. Ma.   Cato Maior

Tatian [Tat.]
Or.   Oratio ad Graecos

Tertullianus [Tert.]
An.   De anima
Ap.   Apologeticus
Carn.   De carne Christi
Ex.   De exhortatione castitatis
Iud.   Adversus Iudeos
Marc.   Adversus Marcionem
Mart.   Ad martyras
Nat.   Ad nationes
Or.   De oratione
Pall.   De pallio
Praescr.   De praescriptione
Spect.   De spectaculis
Test.   De testimonio animae

Theofilus [Theo.]
Ad Autol.   Ad Autolycum

Introduction

"Sirs, what must I do to be saved?"
—Acts 16:30

How should we answer this question? Is not this the reason we reach for the church fathers? Yet, what can writers who lived some eighteen centuries ago really tell us? Tertullian, Justin, Clement, Theophilus, Hippolytus—the very names have about them a musty scent of bygone times. So why do we read them? They are not considered to be geniuses and history textbooks silently bypass their doctrines. The argument that a post-Enlightenment blindness has affected everybody is an oversimplification. When we read the fathers we go through piles of commentaries, we shut our eyes to odd rhetorical flourishes, erudite displays, and unbearably redundant styles, in order to find diamonds from time to time. As Heraclitus used to say, one must dig through a lot of dirt in order to find a bit of gold; this applies to only a small patch of this sort of reading. At first we encounter only dirt. Only later do we get some dirt mixed with gold—a lot of gold.

The fathers are now undone by what used to be their strength. Even though they looked to the heavens, they were firmly planted on the earth. They were not in danger of falling into a cistern like stargazing Thales. They lived in their own here and now. They knew what was *en vogue*. They not only knew the invaluable classics, but also the most fashionable trash—fashionable writers and fashionable barbers, self-proclaimed spiritual gurus, respected authorities, and specialists in self-salvation. There is nothing of the classicist streak in them. They valued the concrete and felt the pulse of their epoch. Even in moments when they ceased to appreciate their own epoch, they never ceased to understand it. Their writing is a conversation, never a lecture; it is a dialogue with a public that must be engaged, convinced, and fortified, a public they belonged to and loved. They do not make *ex cathedra* pronouncements. They engage in a conversation with changing conversation partners, changing contexts, changing diction, changing urgency, but the topic never changes.

This conversation is always concerned with just one thing: Christ, that is, what must be done in order to be saved.

The public they addressed no longer exists. The fashionable problems and outfits also have changed. The writings of the fathers have become one source of knowledge about a forgotten world for those studying their writings in the academy. However, their writings are more important than today's newspapers. Their subjects and stances are still of lasting import. They know our poverty, hunger for the truth, and desire for transformation. These cannot be satisfied by the catacombs of so-called "religious experience," in the quiet of our privacy, or in passing spiritual moods. Their conversions were either all-embracing, or not at all. The effects of these conversions also touched the family, forum, theater, market, and school. The conversions, obviously, could not ignore philosophy, whose masters—like Plato in Raphael's fresco or Jacques-Louis David's monumental Socrates—pointed toward the heavens, toward one's spiritual homeland, thereby calling for conversion and taking up the difficulties of spiritual pilgrimage. But do the philosophers and the prophets direct our gaze toward the same goal? Does philosophy at least lead us partially along the way? Are we nowadays concerned with the same type of conversion, the same type of heaven? What should we do with our philosophical heritage? Should we accept it, reject it, or modify it? What is the role of reason? How is reason related to faith? And what about the relation of revelation to nature? Careful(!), the answer must be clear and concrete, like a chapter from a travel guide (to this world). It should serve salvation. The question is not academic at all! It cannot be an inconsequential and painless theory spawned in the bosom of a long gone Christendom, rather it should address questions posed by everyday life in our pagan, sometimes hostile, and not infrequently dangerous environment.

The preceding list of questions not only grew out of my curiosity about how to answer them, but also from my curiosity about how to ask them. My curiosity was increased by the fact that the fathers lived in times when Christianity, much like today, was not the spiritual center of culture. Is this not one of the main reasons why we are so curious about the experience of Christians from Pre-Constantinian times? Is the present renaissance in patristics not buoyed by the belief that there is an overlap of experience between these two periods? There seems to be a common fate that builds a bridge between them and over those centuries dominated by what used to be Christendom. We want to imbibe the spirit of the origins. We want to look at things from a different perspective by momentarily bracketing-off categories that seem to be necessary only because they are venerable. Yet, to free oneself from the dictates of subsequent opinions is a great temptation, which might actually constrict us and stand in the way of describing the present situation accurately. Yet, we want to listen to people (the great minds!) who had more time to think about how to combine universalism with particularism, who could distinguish the ability to communicate something difficult from speaking in a totally foreign (philosophical) language, and who understood how the necessity of maintaining a specific identity should not be confused with condemning the world. These are the reasons why we return to the fathers today. If nothing else, we want to at least listen to the voices—as authentic as possible, not disfigured—of those who daily faced problems similar to ours. We come back to them in order to listen to them, so that we can at least say whether their work was worth the effort.

I would like to express my gratitude to three outstanding scholars who went through the trouble of reading earlier drafts of this work: Dobrochna Dembińska-Siury, Fr. Wincenty Myszor, and Fr. Tomasz Stępień. Their expert advice is greatly appreciated, and I take responsibility for all the shortcomings of the present work.

I would like to explain one more thing. As you can probably tell, despite the title, this is not a book about Socrates. This book will also not deal with Erasmus, despite the fact that the scholar from Rotterdam coined the phrase "Saint Socrates" in his *Convivium Religiosum*. The topic of this book owes a great deal to an interview I conducted with Juliusz Domański in the Polish monthly *Znak*. This book actually owes much more to Domański's work than what the reader can glean from the bibliography. I would like to thank him for not only giving me the idea for this book's title during our interview, but also for hundreds of conversations in which he generously shared with me with not only his immense knowledge, but also his encouragement and attention. By dedicating this modest little book to him I wholeheartedly thank him for his unswerving generosity and understanding.

1

Whose Athens, Which Jerusalem?

Neither Damned, Nor Saints

DANTE GAVE THE ANCIENT philosophers their own place in the afterlife according to his own set of criteria. Limbo is a strange quasi-hell, a comfortable ante-chamber, "an opening luminous and lofty,"[1] where the philosophers stroll upon a green meadow along with the souls of prophets, ancient heroes, and innocent unbaptized children. Even if they lived sinless lives and achieved much deserved fame, the unbaptized state of the philosophers prevents them from crossing the threshold of heaven and so they spend their ambivalent afterlives in a hellish Arcadia.[2] The positive valuation of philosophy, if it wants to remain Christian, cannot go any further without difficulty. If we do not want to usurp the prerogative of dispensing divine mercy then an empty hell can only be an object of our hope, but never a certainty of our faith. Dante and Erasmus both knew this well, especially since the latter built a fence of reservations around his famous beatification of Socrates.[3] Christ is the principle of Christian iden-

1. Dante, *The Divine Comedy: Hell*, IV.116.

2. See: ibid. IV.31–42, "Thou dost not ask / What spirits these, which thou beholdest, are? / Now will I have thee know, ere thou go farther, // That they sinned not; and if they merit had, / 'Tis not enough, because they had not baptism / Which is the portal of the Faith thou holdest; // And if they were before Christianity, / In the right manner they adored not God; / And among such as these am I myself. // For such defects, and not for other guilt, / Lost are we and are only so far punished, / That without hope we live on in desire."

3. See: Erasmus of Rotterdam, *Convivium religiosum* 683d–e (English translation in: *Familiar Colloquies*, 119) where he writes, "Indeed it was a wonderful elevation of mind in a man, that knew not Christ, nor the Holy Scriptures: And therefore, I can scarce forebear when I read such thing of such men, but cry out, *Sancte Socrates, ora pro nobis*; Saint Socrates, pray for us." This same tone can be found in the great Polish post-Romantic

tity and that is why the problem of salvation outside of Christ, outside of his teaching and sacrifice, is a critical boundary for Christian theology.

However, we should remember that not all Christian thinkers perceived the problem of the salvation of ancient philosophers as something that made them lose sleep. The contempt showered upon pagan sages by thinkers of the caliber of Peter Damian aptly illustrates the range of stances toward philosophy. The picture of noble pagans who march through Elysian Fields to the rhythm of a Dantesque *terza rima* is just one of the many possible answers to the problem of how philosophy relates to revelation. Yet, as suggested by its peculiarity, this might be an especially telling sign of the complicated relations between Athens and Jerusalem, a problem which too often falls prey to tempting oversimplifications.

Juliusz Domański is correct in warning against forcing Christian attitudes toward philosophy into simple binaries.[4] Too often the descriptions of patristic attitudes toward Greek wisdom all too willingly apply the schema of, on the one hand, the party of the sworn enemies of philosophy, and on the other hand, the party of the faithful friends of philosophy. The work of Marcel Simon can serve as one example, out of many, of this tendency. He sets up Justin Martyr as a symbol of the tendency to harmonize, whereas Tertullian is labeled as a representative of anti-philosophical radicalism.[5] But are not such categories wrongheaded? Actually, there is a grain of truth to them. Therefore, the task of the historian who would attempt to precisely delineate the exact principles for discriminating the relationship between theology and philosophy is truly unenviable! Should the guiding principle be the extent and number of Greek quotations, or official declarations of affinity, or the actual fervor for utilizing the heritage of the pagans? Are hidden sympathies more important than involuntary borrowings? We should also ask why the masked Stoicism of Tertullian is less "philosophical" than the ostentatious Platonism of Justin? It would be easy to multiply these types of questions without end. That is not all, the confusion will only multiply if a scholar wants to utilize this dichotomy to demonstrate an "inevitable antagonism" between faith and

---

Cyprian Norwid, who wrote of the all-but-evangelical figure of Epimenides in "Epimenides: A Parable."

4. Domański, "Patrystyczne postawy wobec dziedzictwa antycznego" [Patristic Stands toward the Heritage of Antiquity]. An expanded version of the paper can be found in: *U progu trzeciego tysiaclecia. Czlowiek, nauka, wiara* [On the Threshold of the Third Millenium: Man, Science, Faith], 39–67.

5. Simon, *Cywilizacja wczesnego chrzescijaństwa* [Early Christian Civilization], 143–51.

reason—understood as a supra-historical conflict, that is, independent of the concepts specific to late antiquity.[6]

The Problem of a Pure Christianity

The debate is much more heated than what one would expect given the amount of time separating us from the early church fathers. Is it any wonder? The debate is not about moldy ideas when salvation is at stake. The debate is about whether ties with philosophy poisoned the wells of the Christian tradition. Can we say the diseases of Hellenism were deadly to the life-giving truths of Christ's teaching? These questions cannot be indifferent to Christians. Searching for their resolution directs us into the stream of history. But can we really answer them while using historical tools? We should remember that certain ways of addressing these questions have a way of pigeonholing the historian into the stance of a theologian, if not a prophet, of the revelation that they encounter through their studies.

At the very least since the Reformation laymen have looked with suspicion upon the philosophical robes of Rome. The waning influence of the ancients caused the following questions to emerge: Did the fathers betray revelation when in Chalcedon, or perhaps as early as Constantinople, they expressed the Christian faith with categories borrowed from Greek philosophy, categories not present in the Gospels? Was revelation betrayed by philosophers who only passed for Christians? It is enough to listen to what Martin Luther thinks about it to understand that this debate is about the relevance of the tradition of the ancients.[7]

The name of Adolf Harnack is synonymous with twentieth-century debates about the relationship of philosophy to Christianity. In his seminal work, *What is Christianity?*, Harnack argued that the Christian tradition was effectively Hellenized, and he understood this as a falsification of revelation's core.[8] According to Harnack, the categories of ancient philosophers became

---

6. By postulating the possibility of a more or less non-anachronistic description, I want to avoid regions of dispute redolent with complicated hermeneutical problems. I agree that the ideal of a description free of all anachronisms or interpretations is an intellectual utopia at best—a vain utopia at worst. The final goal of my description is the expression of certain problems in categories that are as universal as possible. The idea of a translator, who through hermeneutical piety refrains from translating, can be our symbol for what I designate as vanity here. Yet, at the same time, I believe that one can and must avoid using categories so inadequate that they blind the researcher to the fundamental distinctions for any given period.

7. See: Gilson, *Heloise and Abelard*, 122–44.

8. E.g., ". . . Roman Catholicism has nothing to do with the Gospel, nay, is in

the constitutive elements of Catholic dogmatics to the detriment of revealed truth's purity.[9] The biggest controversies surrounding Harnack's position did not exclusively concentrate upon the influence of Greek thought in the shaping of Christian tradition. They also concentrated around Harnack's somewhat arbitrary boundary of how much Hellenization is permissible for revelation. It seems that his historical discussion came to be defined by certain *a priori* categories that were unjustifiable on purely historical grounds, even though Harnack appeared to be only concerned with the field of history. It seems that the fervor of his discussion obscured the boundary between historical description and its theological or philosophical interpretation.

It is obvious that revelation, at least to a certain degree, is relativized by the language and culture in which it is expressed. Even the radical other-worldliness of Christianity cannot become a supra-cultural phenomenon. In order to understand the difficulty of establishing restrictive boundaries for the tradition it is enough to recall the choice of the term *logos* as a Johannine theological category, or that the good news was delivered to the world in the native Greek of the philosophers.[10] What historical instruments are available to permit us to establish a clear boundary separating the Hellenization undertaken by Saints Paul and John from those of Justin Martyr?

It would do us well to remember that the first step toward the Hellenization of Christianity was taken long before Christ came into the world, that is, in the work of Hellenization undertaken by the Alexandrian diaspora. After all, the Alexandrian translation of the Pentateuch into the language of Zeno and Plato could not avoid utilizing terminology that had a long history of philosophical usage. The historian can point to the sources and changes of meanings, but we must remember that these tools cannot verify the fact of divine inspiration. The legend about the independent and identical translation of the Bible by seventy-two scholars, which sanctions and baptizes the terminological decisions taken by the translators of the Pentateuch, is beyond the reach of historical criticism. History and literary criticism are obviously very important aids in the study of the Scriptures and revelation. History can equip

---

fundamental contradiction with it." Harnack, *What is Christianity?* 283.

9. "[T]he Church appears as the great insurance society for the ideas of Plato and Zeno" and "Thus was created the future dogmatic in the form which still prevails in the Churches which presupposes the Platonic and Stoic conception of the world long ago overthrown by science." Harnack, *History of Dogma*, Vol. 2, 228–29.

10. "It remains one of the most momentous linguistic convergences in the entire history of the human mind and spirit that the New Testament happens to have been written in Greek—not in the Hebrew of Moses and the prophets, nor in the Aramaic of Jesus and his disciples, nor yet in the Latin of the imperium Romanum, but in the Greek of Socrates and Plato . . . ." Pelikan, *Christianity and Classical Culture*, 3.

the theologian with very important information, however, the question of faith's veracity, or, an evaluation of faith's sources, lies beyond its competence. Christian dogmatics have always considered tradition, besides the Scriptures, to be just such a source, one that comes into being through the inspiration of the Holy Spirit. All who desire to undermine the authenticity of tradition with the help of historical tools take up an entirely vain and cumbersome labor. One cannot derive the criteria of judgment from outside the texts themselves without the risk of falling into a vicious hermeneutic circle. This is why even though Harnack's contribution brought many lively elements into the discussion about the historical dimensions of Christian doctrine, it also led to the insight that the tools of the historian can aid theology, but cannot replace it.[11] The historian is not called to unravel dogmatic questions, because those who speak about orthodoxy are no longer historians, they are theologians. It is obvious that a Christianity essentially free from Hellenization is a theological construct *par excellence*.

The interpretation of Tertullian's work is a practical example of these conundrums. Depending upon the interpreter's opinion about the essence of Christianity, Tertullian is either a prophet of an anti-intellectualism hostile toward the church, or the forerunner of a fiery gospel anti-rationalism.

Let us take a look at the first example. Etienne Gilson is surely preeminent among the thinkers who did not paper over the influence of classical philosophy upon Christianity while defending the authenticity of the teaching passed on by the Christian tradition. Gilson, against Harnack, defended the existence of a Christian philosophy. Referring to Tertullian he said, "It is important for the history of Christian thought that the main enemy of Greek philosophy died outside the Church"; while speaking of Justin Martyr he said, "the one who struggled to gain for Christianity all the advantages of what in Greek culture is good and true, died as a martyr and saint."[12]

11. We can avoid much confusion caused by an inadequate definition of the boundaries of competence for both historians and theologians by proposing two different sets of problems, one for each discipline to address: 1) The following set of problems should be addressed by historians: studying the declared and actual relationship of Christians to philosophy as described in the texts of Christian thinkers, but also the various pagan understandings of philosophy and Christianity, and finally, outlining the historical understandings of the differences and the principles guiding the differences. 2) The theologians should work upon the following: a theological hermeneutic of these phenomena, one that is done with reasonably clear interpretive instruments—without hiding the presuppositions it brings to the table, especially when it comes to analyzing the assumptions of the tradition.

12. See: Gilson, *History of Christian Philosophy in the Middle Ages*. [Translated directly from the Polish edition of the book, Etienne Gilson, *Historia filozofii chrzescijanskiej w wiekach srednich*, 19.] We should note that the view that Tertullian left the church is

Leszek Kolakowski can serve as an example of the second stance. He saw a reflection of the age-old struggle between faith and reason in the writings of the Carthaginian. In Tertullian he saw a Shestovian rebel against reason and a defender of a gospel anti-intellectualism.[13] And so, depending on which perspective upon Christianity one chooses, the one and the same Tertullian constitutes either the personification of what is foreign to the church, or what most fully expresses the gospel.

Someone might say that we can find common ground here. Both authors agree upon the anti-philosophical stance of the Carthaginian. This much is true. This is why both of them will never be able to account for why this declared enemy of everything that is philosophical praises Seneca.[14] bothers to construct philosophical proofs for the existence of God,[15] heartily condemns frivolous faith,[16] and in the work *On the Pallium* calls Christianity itself a philosophy.[17]

Philosophy

The controversy Harnack started, which put the spotlight upon the notion of a pure Christianity, totally ignored the other side of the coin: the essence of the philosophy that Hellenized Christianity. The absence of such a discussion makes it impossible for us to give a serious answer as to why the very same authors could condemn philosophy and at the same time use it to their purposes at will. Furthermore, they also called Christianity a philosophy! When I say "a serious answer" I mean one that does not reduce these difficulties to a lack of consequence, or something like Gospel-marketing strategies of the ancient Christians.

In the introduction to his monumental *The Spirit of Mediaeval Philosophy* Gilson, somewhat in passing, formulates the principle dividing philosophy and religion, which according to him protected Christianity from betraying its essence: "The incarnation and death of Christ on the cross found themselves at the center of the world's history thanks to Christianity's concentration upon on the living person of Christ, it is less a speculative point of view upon reality

widely questioned today, for example in David Rankin, *Tertullian and the Church*.

13. Kolakowski, *Religion: If There Is No God*, 128.

14. Tert., *An.* 20.1.

15. For example, in the short work *The Soul's Testimony*.

16. Tert., *Marc.* 5.1.1.

17. Tert., *Pall.* 6.2.

than a way of life. Not a philosophy, but a religion."[18] I would like to turn our attention not to the definition of Christianity, but to the definition of philosophy, which is identified with a speculative gaze upon reality. Furthermore, it is somewhat negatively identified with not being a way of salvation, not being a way of life.

Gilson utilizes in his polemic with Harnack a fixed definition of philosophy, understood as a purely theoretical or epistemological activity. Today we know that this is a caricature of ancient philosophy. Thanks to studies on the nature of the philosophical enterprise written by scholars such as Juliusz Domański in Poland and Pierre Hadot in France, we know without a doubt that ancient philosophy was a "way of life."[19] Moreover, according to Hadot, "If we disregard, for the moment, the monastic usage of the word *philosophia*, we can say that philosophy in the Middle Ages had become a purely theoretical and abstract activity. It was no longer a way of life."[20] We should add that it is precisely this understanding of philosophy—scholastic in its roots—that Gilson projects onto the reality that constituted the intellectual milieu of early Christianity.

An entirely different answer can be expected from those whom we can call "oversimplifiers." What I mean is those who hold an interpretation of the relationship between ancient Christianity and philosophy as being a collision between a faith that derives its reasons from revelation and a reason (rationality, philosophy) independent of the authority of religion. Without going into matters that will be covered later in this book, we can say that it would be extremely difficult to find real-life evidence for the existence of both sides of this confrontation as characterized in these two ideal models.

Both of the positions described above ignore the philosophy that ancient Christianity encountered: a philosophy that was more than anything a "way

18. Gilson, *Historia filozofii chrzescijanskiej w wiekach srednich*, 8. [Translated directly from the Polish edition of the book—trans.]

19. See: Domański, *Erazm i filozofia. Studium o koncepcji filozofii Erazma z Rotterdamu* [Erasmus and Philosophy: A Study of Erasmus of Rotterdam's Concept of Philosophy], especially the chapter "Osobliwosci i paradoksy filozoficznego zycia" [The Peculiarities and Paradoxes of the Philosophical Life], 20–90; Domański, "«Scholastyczne» i «humanistyczne» pojecie filozofii" [The "Scholastic" and "Humanist" Conceptions of Philosophy], 8–24; Domański, "Metamorfozy pojecia filozofii" [Metamorphoses in Understandings of Philosophy], 3–19. And for Hadot: *Philosophy as a Way of Life*, 79–144 and 264–76; *What is Ancient Philosophy?*; *The Inner Citadel*, especially 35–53.

20. Hadot, *Philosophy as a Way of Life*, 270. Hadot directly addresses his debt to Gilson in ibid., 277. For Domański's criticism of Gilson refer to his afterword to the Polish edition of *Philosophy as a Way of Life*, 255–56 and also see: Domański, "Quelques observations sur l'attitude d'Erasme envers la philosophie" [Some Observations on the Attitude of Erasmus towards Philosophy].

of life." In contemporary times, for several reasons, the spirit and practice of ancient philosophical schools is more readily found in monasteries than universities—especially when we take into consideration the constant effort of moral and intellectual exercises (*askesis*) that transformed the knowledge and lives of authentic philosophical adepts.[21] Many phenomena that we are inclined to recognize as *par excellence* religious today were actually decisive for demonstrating the philosophical nature of ancient Christianity.[22] Additionally, Werner Jaeger notes, "Even the word 'conversion' stems from Plato, for adopting a philosophy meant a change in life in the first place."[23] Philosophical schools played such an important role in the ancient world because they did help to explain worldly phenomena, but also "[s]econdly—and this is a point of cardinal importance—the schools offered a life with a scheme. One of the terms for a school of philosophy, whatever its kind, is *agoge*, which means way of teaching and way of living."[24] We should also keep in mind that it was not only the Christians who willingly called themselves philosophers, but those pagans involved in polemics against them called the Christians philosophers as well.[25] This was made possible by the convergence of interests, goals, and methods of the spiritual life. It was likewise connected to the widespread authority afforded to spiritual masters,[26] but also, because of an entirely different approach (from our contemporary perspective) toward the key issue of the relation between faith and reason.

In all ancient philosophical schools the element of faith, with the exception of the skeptics, constituted the starting point on the way toward happiness, virtue, and the fullness of knowledge. Philosophy, understood as the path toward perfection, promised the fullness of knowledge only at the end of one's philosophizing—this was the case for students of Plato, Aristotle, Chrysippus, or Epicurus. Philosophy involved faith in the authenticity of the guidelines that led one to the goal, that is, faith in the correctness of the advice given by the spiritual director (*kathegemon,* Greek for one who leads, who shows the

---

21. Hadot, *What is Ancient Philosophy?*, 239.

22. Kelly, *Early Christian Doctrines*, 23. There Kelly discusses the philosophical environment in which Christianity emerged as one where, "Philosophy was the deeper religion of most intelligent people."

23. Jaeger, *Early Christianity and Greek Paideia*, 8; See: Meeks, *The Origins of Christian Morality*, 23.

24. Nock, *Conversion*, 167.

25. Jaeger, *Early Christianity and Greek Paideia*, 32.

26. Dembińska-Siury, "Filozoficzne duszpasterstwo. O religijnej misji Sokratesa" [Philosophical Priesthood: The Religious Mission of Socrates], 208–18; I. Hadot, "The Spiritual Guide," 436–52.

path). Both of these factors were integral elements of the philosophical life.[27] Before we hastily take the accusations of Celsus or Galen that the Christians, "believe without rational thought,"[28] as the paradigm for the battle of Greek philosophy against Christianity, we should first, for example, pick up Lucian's *Hermotimus* where similar objections are voiced by the skeptic against, more or less, nearly every ancient philosophical school.[29]

Even if the extreme egalitarianism of the church might have greatly multiplied the accusations that Christians cared less about the intellectual development of their pupils than other schools, the claim that Christians based their lives upon faith can be more properly understood within the context of the controversy between the skeptics and the academics, that is, a controversy at the heart of philosophy itself. The claim that the heart of the discussion between philosophy and faith was constituted by differences between skeptics and Christians requires an absurd concession, namely, that the skeptics—not, for example, the Platonists, Peripatetics, or Stoics—represented the true spirit of ancient philosophy and the mainline ancient philosophical understanding of reason.

Whether one likes it or not, the situation of the early Christians cannot be transposed upon the discussions between Peter Damian and Abelard or Shestov and Husserl. If in the name of some arbitrarily selected definitions of philosophy and reason we take away ancient Christianity's right to use these two concepts, then we should also consider whether we are not at the same time involuntarily depriving other ancient philosophical schools of those two concepts; we should also remember that these very philosophical schools converted their pupils by utilizing the concept of reason whose definition depended upon the categories of causality, nature, and teleology.

Three Questions

I realize that I am sticking out my neck by making another attempt to answer Tertullian's question about what Athens and Jerusalem have in common. The fact that I limit myself to only several early Christian thinkers does not substantially change this situation. My decision to embrace this risky undertaking is based upon my belief in the merits of taking up three distinct yet interconnected questions.

27. Nock, *Conversion*, 181.

28. Origenes, *Cels.* I.9–11, 12.

29. Lucianus, *Herm.*, 85.

Right from the beginning Christians were convinced about the existence of numerous convergences between certain positions of the philosophers and the truths of revelation. Saint Paul's confrontation with the philosophers (Acts 17:22–31) is the best example. In a short speech at the Areopagus, which did not ignore the substantial uniqueness of Christianity, Saint Paul made use of a surprisingly long list of theses Christianity holds in common with some ancient philosophical schools. The following generations of Christians would expand this list of convergences to impressive dimensions, filling it out with subtle analyses and commentaries full of numerous reservations. Independently of how the presence of these overlaps was interpreted, nobody doubted their existence. It was impossible to ignore the question of their origins, even though for many thinkers they appeared to be too inconsequential to cast an appreciative eye upon pagan philosophy. Therefore, it is impossible to avoid asking about the origin of the pearls that can be found outside the church and the question of how they are related to revelation, even for those who hold a very antagonistic stance toward the philosophical achievements of the Greeks. Were not some philosophical theses, as the Alexandrian school of theology thought, simply stolen from the Jewish Bible?[30] Could it be that while traveling to Egypt Plato encountered the teachings of Moses? The earnestness of this hypothesis does not really deserve more than a polite smile.[31] It mainly reveals the civilizational aspirations of ancient Jews and Christians, but it also reveals the gravity of the problem facing ancient Christians.[32]

30. Philo listed three sources of the truths found in Greek philosophy: borrowings, reason, and divine inspiration. See: Daniélou, *Gospel Message and Hellenistic Culture*, 40. Daniélou shows how Philo's arguments were adopted by the Apologists.

31. However extravagant this theory appears today Henry Chadwick is correct to note that, "it must also be recognized from a strictly historical viewpoint our superior smile is a grossly unimaginative anachronism." Chadwick, *Early Christian Thought and the Classical Tradition*, 14.

32. The belief that the Greeks borrowed their wisdom from the Bible was born among the Alexandrian diaspora when Aristobulus and Philo who—much like the early Christians later—were amazed by their discovery of Greek wisdom. The writings of these Jewish thinkers passed on this conviction both to Christians and even some pagans, who like the Pythagorean Numenius of Apamea asked rhetorically: "For what is Plato, but Moses speaking in Attic Greek?" See: Clem. Al., *Str.* I.XXII.150.4, ANF2, 335. [Henceforth all citations from the 10-volume *Ante-Nicene Fathers* series from the Christian Publishing Company (1885) will be cited starting with the author and standard abbreviated title of the patristic text, followed by ANF plus the number of the volume, and finally the number of the page(s) cited. The *Nicene and Post-Nicene Fathers* series will cited the same way, but with a NPNF. —trans.]. Proclaiming the primacy of the Bible over philosophy, depending upon the apologetic needs, is utilized to explain similarities and to point out pagan perversions of the original truth. I am convinced that something greater is at play here than just than the hopes of discrediting the Greeks by the monotheistic upstarts, or

Adjudicating the analogies between philosophy and Christianity requires an attempt to distill and answer the following questions: How are we to explain these similarities? Does their existence seriously challenge the radical uniqueness of the teaching revealed by Jesus Christ? Whence comes the truth outside of revelation? When relying only upon his own powers is man capable of knowing any of the truth revealed to Christians? Is it the case that, despite the unambiguous teaching of the Epistle to the Corinthians, the wisdom of the world can have anything to do with the wisdom of God? Can one speak of some kind of universal or natural revelation that God gave to all reasonable creatures? Did God not make the wisdom of the world foolishness (1 Cor 1:20)? "Certain of our brethren," wrote Augustine, "are amazed when they hear or read that Plato had an understanding of God which, as they see, is in many respects consistent with the truth of our religion."[33] If, as Aristotle claims, philosophy is born in wonder, then his statement also refers to this strange coincidence. It simply cannot be ignored. The problem of the sources of truth leads straight into the question of how reason and revelation are related—and to the very core of philosophy.

This is our starting point. Now we will address and attempt to answer the three main problems outlined above. If we agree that the pagans came to know some part of the truth then: 1) We must ask how it happened, 2) what portion of the truth they did come to know, 3) whether philosophical knowledge of this truth is needed after the fullness of truth was revealed by God. Above all, the first problem is a question about the causes of the possible

---

that it all is a pious masquerade to cover up the Hellenization of revelation. All of this leads to the question about the possibilities of human reason when faced with God's transcendence. Is the concept of theft an answer that is dear to all those who had a low appraisal of natural knowledge? The matter is not that simple. Essentially the notion of theft—or to put it more kindly, borrowing—is capable of explaining overlaps that clearly go beyond what is given to natural reason. This is why its rejection forces one to put more emphasis on the capabilities of natural reason. Saint Augustine, who criticizes the theory of borrowing in *The City of God* (VII.XI), answers the question of where Plato got his knowledge of God with the words of Romans 1:19–21. However, in practice, it is difficult to ascribe to the theory of borrowing some type of unambiguous understanding of the relationship between faith and reason. It is not a necessary consequence of any of the positions toward reason or philosophy. It is used by enthusiasts of philosophy such as Clement in the *Stromata* (I.XXII.150.1–3), but sometimes both understandings are used simultaneously, for example, in Justin Martyr—who sees as borrowings only those elements whose discovery seems impossible by way of natural reason. See: Iust., *Apol.* I.44.8–9; 59–60; Tat., *Or.* 1.35–40; Min. Fel., *Oct.* 20.1; 34.5; Tert., *Ap.* 19; Clem. Al., *Str.* I.XVI.80.5. Also see: Pelikan, *The Emergence of the Catholic Tradition*, 33–34; Daniélou, *Gospel Message and Hellenistic Culture*, 46–47.

33. Augustinus, *De civ. Dei* VIII.XI.1.

overlaps between the teachings of the pagans and revelation, that is, the matter of mutual relations between pagan philosophy, reason, nature, and revelation. The second problem constitutes an evaluation of the factual range of similarities, that is, a question about how much truth can be found in philosophy. The third problem pertains to the issue of selection and adoption, that is, a question about the usefulness of philosophy and ways of utilizing pagan philosophy in Christian teaching and life. These are the three domains which, as it seems to me, will help us to best characterize the stance of Christians toward philosophy and, at the same time, they will help us avoid accusing the theologians of ignorance, chicanery, lack of consequence, exuberance in rhetorical enthusiasm, or even psychological disorders.[34]

34. Jung, *Psychological Types*, 11.

2

What do Athens and Jerusalem Have in Common?

When Leibniz set out on the search for truth, he always armed himself with the principle of contradiction and the principle of sufficient reason, just as, in his own words, a captain of a ship arms himself on setting out to sea with a compass and maps. These two principles Leibniz called his invincible soldiers. But if one or the other of these principles is shaken, how is truth to be sought? There is something here about which one feels troubled and even frightened.[1]

—LEV SHESTOV

Euthyphro's Dilemma

I AM CONVINCED THAT many misinterpretations of early Christian thinkers emerge from identifying their stance toward pagan philosophy with a general stance toward reason. I am convinced this identification is false. The relationship of Christianity to philosophy, and its relation to reason, are two entirely different things, not only in light of Saint Paul's epistles, but also the works of Tertullian, Hippolytus, or Epiphanus. The question of the extent of humanity's natural knowledge, especially whether people can come to know God on their own, cannot be reduced to the question of faith's relationship to the positive historical instances of philosophy among the Greeks and Romans. Above all, the wonder caused by the discovery of truths scattered throughout the teachings of ancient sages put Christians face to face with the problem of natural knowledge, and only secondarily with the issue of the value of its fruits. Even

1. Shestov, *Athens and Jerusalem*, 50–51.

though the assessment of natural reason constituted the bedrock of evaluating the philosophical heritage of the pagans (it precedes it in an obvious way), the evaluation of reason did not have to go hand-in-hand with an evaluation of the achievements of Plato, Socrates, Zeno, or Epicurus. One can be a Christian rationalist and still deprecate the philosophers for their meager use of reason. One can also have a critical evaluation of human knowledge and at the same time sincerely admire philosophy for its extraordinary achievements. This divergence will increase when we remember that the philosophies and the philosophers encountered by early Christians did not practice a purely theoretical enterprise. The schools required total engagement from their adepts. They called them to conversion and spiritual transformation (*metanoia*) and therefore they led to competing ways (*agogai*) of life. All of this resulted in competition between the philosophical schools, and eventually to competition between the philosophical schools and Christians.

It is already difficult to find an identification of reason and philosophy in Saint Paul.[2] It is true that the immense power of the paradoxical phrases from 1 Corinthians—where the wisdom of God (the foolishness of the cross) is confronted with the wisdom of the world—inclines one to put the entirety of human knowledge under the shadow of an immense question mark (this applies equally to reason and its philosophical fruits).[3] Yet, the assertions that there is no compromise between God's wisdom and the wisdom of the world and that revelation is foolishness in the eyes of the wise of the world do not mean that all human wisdom is preemptively condemned by revelation. After all, such a stance would not only force us to ignore the philosophical tradition of paradox, but it would also require us to bracket off the theses of the Epistle to the Romans about the possibility of natural knowledge and the reliability of the summons of conscience, "For what can be known about God is evident

---

2. I discuss this more thoroughly on pages 31–61 of the Polish edition of *The Archparadox of Death*. A translation of this book by Artur Sebastian Rosman is forthcoming via Peter Lang Publishers.

3. "For Christ did not send me to baptize but to preach the gospel, and not with the wisdom of human eloquence, so that the cross of Christ might not be emptied of its meaning. The message of the cross is foolishness to those who are perishing, but to us who are being saved it is the power of God. For it is written: 'I will destroy the wisdom of the wise, and the learning of the learned I will set aside.' Where is the wise one? Where is the scribe? Where is the debater of this age? Has not God made the wisdom of the world foolish? For since in the wisdom of God the world did not come to know God through wisdom, it was the will of God through the foolishness of the proclamation to save those who have faith. For Jews demand signs and Greeks look for wisdom, but we proclaim Christ crucified, a stumbling block to Jews and foolishness to Gentiles, but to those who are called, Jews and Greeks alike, Christ the power of God and the wisdom of God" (1 Cor 1:17–24). *The New American Bible* will be used throughout this volume [—trans.].

to them, because God made it evident to them. Ever since the creation of the world, his invisible attributes of eternal power and divinity have been able to be understood and perceived in what he has made" (Rom 1:19–20). This was also written by Saint Paul, but in praise of natural reason, by utilizing standards of rationality that were the common property of nearly all ancient philosophy. And if that is not enough, he adds, "For when the Gentiles who do not have the law by nature observe the prescriptions of the law, they are a law for themselves even though they do not have the law. They show that the demands of the law are written in their hearts, while their conscience also bears witness and their conflicting thoughts accuse or even defend them" (Rom 2:14–15). These passages from Saint Paul obviously leave no doubt that the apostle is speaking about imperfect knowledge and a voice of conscience so faint that it would be an improbable basis for even a relatively just life. The universal capabilities for reasoning and acting morally constitute a sufficient basis for taking responsibility for one's acts, including for those individuals who have not been directly addressed by the Word of God, even if it is only the glory of the truth revealed in Christ that opens up the way toward perfection to humanity.

Are we not overvaluing the rationalist intentions of the Epistle to the Romans? Is such a tendency a sign of corruption by Hellenism, which is based upon giving reason rights that for many centuries made faith the prisoner of scholastic pride? Does not Paul merely say that the pagans have no foundations for expecting to be let off the hook? After all, they have wasted the natural gifts of reason and conscience. Does this gift have any value after Christ's revelation of the fullness of truth? Is not the Christian teaching a call to religious sovereignty, an appeal to a faith that will cast its demands upon a reason which would like to entrap the Living Truth within a net of philosophical necessities? Is this not the starting point for the tradition that goes all the way to Peter Damian and later Ockham? It is a tradition that makes truth and the good dependent upon the will of God, a tradition that presents an irresolvable conflict between the truth of the faith and the dead truths of reason; the tree of life versus the tree of knowledge. Does not belief in God mean trusting God to such a degree that allows us to suspend all convictions and calculations? Is it not the true faith—as Kierkegaard wrote in *Fear and Trembling* while discussing the sacrifice of Isaac—an absurd path, not a reasonable one?[4] It seems that faith in the omnipotence of God should lead us to conclude that the rules of reason are provisional. The very same rules that reason in its limitations posits as necessary and unchanging. After all, the rules of logic and ethical

---

4. Kierkegaard, *Fear and Trembling*, 65: "He believed on the strength of the absurd, for there could be no question of human calculation."

norms that are blasphemously regarded as universal and necessary cannot confine God. Is this not the teaching proclaimed by the great Christians to the world, Christians such as Tertullian who audaciously proclaimed *certum est, quia impossibile* [it is certain because it is impossible]? Was not this teaching undermined by the followers of Justin Martyr who were mesmerized by Greek philosophy? These are not vain questions, however, we must explore whether they are well put.

Asking about the competence of human reason clearly reopens one of the most important controversies that have accompanied Christianity from its birth. The following are at stake: on the one hand, the relationship between reason and nature, on the other, the relationship between God's transcendence and omnipotence. These are the fundamental questions for defining the character of what we will call "Christian philosophy."

If revelation reveals the necessary order of reality (one that exists objectively) and if this order is not fully knowable naturally, then the rules of Christian teaching cannot be proven, yet they are absolute, that is, unchanging and universally binding. It is a given that some part of revelation, which Christians label as a mystery, always remains paradoxical to human reason. Here paradox is strictly defined as inaccessible to human reason, rather than contrary to the absolute laws of thinking and acting that are available to us. The paradoxicality of mystery is a sign of our finitude, rather than a sign of the provisional character of the rules of thinking and acting available to reason. Independently of how deeply paradoxical and unintelligible the mystery of God's love shows itself to be in the sacrifice of Christ, or, in the mystery of the Trinity, its truth in no way disturbs the moral and logical laws known through purely natural means. This means that it is not the mystery that is unintelligible, instead our reason is not capable of knowing the mystery, which can be only fully explicated in the light of knowing the knowledge of the fullness of the absolute order, which remains inaccessible to us.

The Christian can direct his life according to pointers that he does not comprehend, yet still be convinced that he is living rationally. However, he need not make a sacrifice of reason, because he believes that he is properly using reason, and is inching ever closer to its proper goal.

Conversely, conceptions of revelation that cross out nature, a God who proclaims to humanity laws that contradict the ones presiding over human thinking and being, destroys any correlation between natural reason and the divine will. The discontinuity that appears between God and the world in such theologies is permanent. They do not allow for talking about the boundaries of knowledge, the problem is no longer finitude, but the radical alterity of God's wisdom toward human reason. The matter is rooted in an understanding of

God's nature and transcendence, and is best expressed in the question: should God be constrained or limited by the laws ruling reality, or conversely, are these laws completely dependent on his will? In some cases the positing of God's radical alterity is transformed into an obligation of sacrificing reason (*sacrificium intellectus*) and all the laws that govern knowledge and thinking. If God decides that 2 x 2 = 5, or, that murder and denouncing one's parents is laudable, then it will be so. When the laws revealed by God are dependent upon God's will, then they simultaneously stop being necessary and unchanging, however, in concert with the sovereign will of their Creator, they are both real and binding. According to the proud opponents of necessity this formulation solves the dilemmas of Plato's *Euthyphro*—does God love what is good or is what God loves the good?

Tertullian's Rationalism

The understanding of transcendence presented in this way is often attributed to the thinker who—this is significant—passes as the father of Latin theology. It is difficult to doubt that some of Tertullian's statements play into this assumption. Tertullian's well-known statements forcefully contrast philosophy and Christianity as two mutually exclusive realities. In the famous phrases from the *Apology* he denies all similarities and any commingling between the philosopher and Christian, the pupil of Greece and the student of heaven, the friend of error and his enemy.[5] In the *Prescription Against the Heretics* these antinomies are filled out with two more, Athens versus Jerusalem and the Academy versus the church.[6] The stereotyping of Tertullian as a Christian who tends toward annihilating reason by stressing the paradoxicality of revelation is also borne out by a popular fragment from *De carne Christi*, where the Carthaginian derives the authenticity of the Son of God's death through its absurdity and the certainty of the resurrection through its impossibility.[7] Yet, one needs the blindness of a Shestov to not notice that philosophy, Greece, attachment to error, Athens, and the Academy need not be (and they are not!) synonyms for natural reason, but rather historical examples of its compromise. Being anti-philosophical is not the same as being anti-rational.[8] Tertullian,

5. See: Tert., *Ap.* 46.18.

6. See: Tert., *Praescr.* 7.9. See: Hier., *Epist.* 22.29, NPNF 2.6, 35: "For what communion has light with darkness? And what concord has Christ with Belial? (2 Cor 6:14–15) How can Horace go with the Psalter, Virgil with the Gospels, Cicero with the apostle?"

7. See: Tert., *Carn.* 5.4.

8. Osborn, while discussing the above lists from the *Prescription* and from *On the Flesh* notes that, "These two claims have become slogans in fideist alternatives to the

with all of his considerable conviction, merely says that philosophy, only up to his day, represents falsehood. That emphatically does not mean that reason cannot even touch a sliver of the truth. Furthermore, he adds in *The Soul's Testimony* that positive historical philosophy does not represent nature at all. In the mind of Tertullian there is no quarrel between revelation and nature.[9] If there is any quarrel proclaimed by Tertullian, it is the conflict between nature and positive historical philosophy. Tertullian makes war against a philosophy that falsifies nature; he makes war in the name of both reason, nature, *and revelation*.

Pure nature is in its essence Christian, that is, we discover within it an order that is not contrary to revelation. And so Tertullian, just like his intellectual contemporaries, is ready to treat the *kosmos* as a proof for the existence of God.[10] The position Paul expressed in the Epistle to the Romans is upheld by Tertullian—reason is not the object of his critique, but the use philosophers have made of reason.[11] However, we should add that Tertullian's Christian contemporaries added very little to the ideas of the great Diogenes of Apollonia that were developed by the Platonists and Stoics.[12] Clement, bishop of Rome, in a letter dated to the end of the first century reveals the majestic order of all things in a hymn that proclaims the greatness of the Creator as an example truly worthy of imitation for Christians.[13] We should note that this hymn is intended as a spiritual exercise for believers in a Corinth torn apart by theological controversies. Contemplation of the order visible in the cosmos in which God's might realizes itself is meant as a medicine for the soul and an

---

Enlightenment where they have each acquired a meaning which is foreign to Tertullian. . . . [It is] necessary to show that Tertullian was not a fideist. Not only did he never say 'credo quia absurdum,' but he never meant anything like it." Osborn, *Tertullian*, 27–28.

9. Osborn, *The Emergence of Christian Theology*, 233–34.

10. See: Tert., *Ap.* 17.1–4.

11. Shestov's polemics with Gilson set out a brave thesis, namely, that in Paul and Tertullian we are not so much dealing with a rejection of reason, but with a rejection of *Greek* reason and the proclamation of a radically new model of rationality. "Yet if Isaiah and Saint Paul are right, Tertullian's declaration [this obviously must be *On the Flesh of Christ*, 5—D.K.] must serve as the introduction or prolegomena to the organon of the Judeo-Christian philosophy, which was called to proclaim to the world the new notion, completely ignored up until then, of 'created truth.' We must, before everything else, reject the basic categories of Greek thought, tear out from our being all the postulates of our 'natural knowledge' and our 'natural morality.'" Shestov, *Athens and Jerusalem*, 288. The most standard hermeneutic methods will always lead us to the conclusion that Tertullian's conceptions of nature and reason reject the shackles imposed upon them by the Greeks.

12. Armstrong and Markus, *Christian Faith and Greek Philosophy*, 9.

13. See: Clem. Rom., *Epist.* 19.2—20.11.

example of the order and unity that should reign between those who follow Christ.[14] There is no better argument for the non-contradiction of nature and revelation.

In all honesty, we should also note that for members of the early church the ability to intellectually see the face of God in nature and the laws created by him—laws that simultaneously govern human life and all of nature—was considered to be an insight that was not necessarily accessible universally. I believe Clement himself would incline toward the understanding that only Christians possess this view of nature in full, and that revelation is a precondition for natural knowledge of God.[15] However, the later statement of Saint Theophilus, "Consider, O man, His works"[16] was generally taken to be an expression of the confidence in the universal capability of human reason to discover the existence of the Creator and the laws of a righteous life. Minucius Felix takes up precisely that position in his *Octavius* in chapters 17 and 18. We should also remember his attack upon up the mechanistic and atomistic positions of Democritus when we read him. Then we will not be surprised by the fact that his contemporaries gave him the nickname Cicero, especially when we read fragments such as this one, "[T]hey who deny that this furniture of the whole world was perfected by the divine reason, and assert that it was heaped together by certain fragments casually adhering to each other, seem to me not to have either mind or sense, or, in fact, even sight itself."[17]

---

14. Jaeger, *Early Christianity and Greek Paideia*, 12–25.

15. The following fragment in Clem. Rom., *Epist. 36.2*, ANF 1, 14–15, leads us to this conclusion: "By Him we look up to the heights of heaven. By Him we behold, as in a glass, His immaculate and most excellent visage. By Him are the eyes of our hearts opened. By Him our foolish and darkened understanding blossoms up anew towards His marvelous light. By Him the Lord has willed that we should taste of immortal knowledge, who, being the brightness of His majesty, is by so much greater than the angels, as He has by inheritance obtained a more excellent name than they." When reading this fragment we should remember that Clement is not actually discussing the topic of the possibility of a theoretical discovery of God's existence through his works. Instead he is discussing eternal wisdom, that is, one that requires a total conversion of human existence. For readers of the Old Testament (in the Greek version) faith as a condition of knowledge is nothing new: "If you do not stand firm in your faith, you will not understand at all" says Isaiah (7:9).

16. Theo., *Ad Autol.* I.6.1, ANF 2, 90.

17. See: Min. Fel., *Oct.* 17.3, ANF 4, 182. See: Arist., *Apol.* 1. In the work *The Nature of the Gods* Cicero wrote "I am thinking for instance of the fallacious theory of Democritus—or was it his predecessor Leucippus?—which would have us believe only in minute particles, some rough, some smooth . . . and that from these particles have been created the heavens and the earth, not by any natural force but merely by a sort of accidental collision!" Cic., *Nat. deor.* I.24.66, 95–96.

Tertullian, who was accused of extremism, not only approves, but creatively develops a way of thinking that confirms the substantial unity of the natural and revealed, that is, God's whole order. "Would you have the proof from the works of His hands, so numerous and so great, which both contain you and sustain you, which minister at once to your enjoyment, and strike you with awe; or would you rather have it from the testimony of the soul itself?"[18] asks the Carthaginian in the seventeenth chapter of his *Apology*. In his argument taken from the "testimony of the soul" Tertullian leans upon a whole arsenal of medical metaphors, which had an obvious philosophical provenance in his time, and have served from time immemorial to underscore the difference between nature and the fallen, therefore unnatural, everyday experience. The soul whose testimony is the basis for Tertullian's argument was once flabbergasted, but recovered its health as if from an illness. The testimony is framed by commonplace sayings such as, "What God gives," "God sees," "I commend to God" that reveal for Tertullian the presence in the soul of knowledge that is essentially in accord with Christian teaching, even if for the most part this knowledge is usually obscured by our "illness." The soul is, as Tertullian claims, *naturaliter christiana*, meaning, it is naturally oriented toward God, "O noble testimony of the soul by nature Christian! Then, too, in using such words as these, it looks not to the Capitol, but to the heavens. It knows that there is the throne of the living God, as from Him and from thence itself came down."[19] This concept of the soul's testimony, which was developed during the writing of *The Apology*, seemed to be so profitable to Tertullian that he wrote a whole separate work upon it. One must admit that reading this text forces one to revise one of the most stubborn prejudices about early Christianity: the picture of Tertullian as the incarnation of the conflict between revealed faith and natural reason.

The following list from Tertullian's *The Apology* details some of the main causes and symptoms of the illness that disfigure the soul's knowledge: crushing imprisonment by the body, the limitations caused by a bad upbringing, dissolution through sensuality, desire, and serving false gods.[20] In *The Soul's Testimony* the accusations are directed against philosophy itself, which is singled out as the main corrupter of natural knowledge. Tertullian calls the soul to the witness stand in order to vouch for the truth of the Christian claim, "[S]tand forth and give thy witness. But I call thee not as when, fashioned in schools, trained in libraries, fed in Attic academies and porticoes, thou belchest wisdom. I address thee simple, rude, uncultured and untaught, such

18. Tert., *Ap.* 17.4, ANF 3, 32.

19. Ibid. XVII.5, 32.

20. Ibid. XVII.5, 32.

as they have thee who have thee only; that very thing of the road, the street, the work-shop, wholly. I want thine inexperience, since in thy small experience no one feels any confidence."[21] One can clearly see the ideal of an intelligent noble savage did not originate in the mind of Jean-Jacques Rousseau. In Tertullian this idea certainly corresponds with his concept of a universal, foundational, unwritten, and universal natural law passed on to every human being through Adam and Eve, who received it before the fall (original sin is the breaking of this law).[22]

The very idea of a witness of a pure soul might have been suggested by the famous experiment of Psammetichus. The future king of Egypt conducted an experiment that would help him discover what the natural or first language might be. He put a newborn child in the care of a nanny whose tongue was cut out to make sure that the first word uttered by the child would not be one it came to know aurally.[23] Tertullian must have taken to the idea of a natural language, because in his discussion of this episode in the first book of *Ad Nationes* he merely questions the methods used in the macabre experiment, rather than the possibility of reaching the origins.[24]

21. Tert., *Test.* 1, ANF 3, 175.

22. See: Tert., *Iud.* 2, ANF 3, 152–53 where we read: "For why should God, the founder of the universe, the Governor of the whole world, the Fashioner of humanity, the Sower of universal nations be believed to have given a law through Moses to one people, and not be said to have assigned it to all nations? . . . For in the beginning of the world He gave to Adam himself and Eve a law, that they were not to eat of the fruit of the tree planted in the midst of paradise. . . . For in this law given to Adam we recognize in embryo all the precepts which afterwards sprouted forth when given through Moses. . . . In short, before the Law of Moses written in stone-tables, I contend that there was a law unwritten, which was habitually understood naturally, and by the fathers was habitually kept. For whence was Noah 'found righteous,' if in his case the righteousness of a natural law had not preceded? Whence was Abraham accounted 'a friend of God,' if not on the ground of equity and righteousness, (in the observance) of a natural law? . . . Whence we understand that God's law was anterior even to Moses, and was not first (given) in Horeb, nor in Sinai and in the desert, but was more ancient; (existing) first in paradise . . . ." On the content of the law see: Pelikan, *The Emergence of the Catholic Tradition*, 32 and Osborn, *Tertullian*, 138, 155.

23. Supposedly the Phrygian word *bekos* (bread) was the first word uttered by the baby.

24. See: Tert., *Nat.* 1.8 where he proves that the nanny could in no way survive the removal of her tongue. In a version recorded by Herodotus [*The Histories*, II.2, 96] the children were raised by two shepherds who remained silent, "the Greeks have various improbable versions of the stories," here Herodotus probably has Pindar and Hecataeus in mind, "such as that Psammetichus had the children brought up by women whose tongues he had cut out."

We should abstract from the textual sources by noting that Tertullian is referring to a certain intellectual tradition that presupposes the existence of an undisturbed, primary, and therefore fundamental, experience of reality written into language. We can see this in Plato's *Cratylus* in the myth of the name-givers (*onomatothetai*) who gave things their proper names by adequately describing their natures through their given names.[25] According to the myth time has corrupted both the language and our ability for direct knowledge. Therefore, the work of the name-givers hidden within the original words is our only access to the real nature of things. This theory was adopted and given a biblical background by Philo of Alexandria. The myth of an original language is expressed by him in a passage elaborating the existence of an authentic language that was used by Adam and Eve in Eden. Its epistemological essence is expressed by the scene in Genesis where Adam names all the animals paraded before him by God. These were names that "reveal[ed] in an excellent fashion the individual characteristics of their subjects." Philo's discussion assumes this pure knowledge as not contaminated by the consequences of original sin: "After all, the rational nature in his soul was still uncorrupted, and not a single weakness or disease or passion had found its way in. So he took in wholly unblemished impressions of things material and immaterial, and made appellations that were accurate, taking aim in excellent fashion at what was revealed, so that their natures were pronounced and understood at the very same time."[26] In Herodotus this tradition appears in the form of a myth about an original and natural language that allows one to identify the most authentic of all existing languages. Whereas in Tertullian the problem of uncontaminated knowledge—one of the ultimate questions of philosophy—leads to a critique directed at philosophy.

This originarity and primacy is twofold. First of all, the colloquial speech of simple people is inscribed with the original knowledge of the soul, which is, above all, natural and therefore true. Second, this language is, as we would say today, pre-cultural. This means it owes nothing to culture or philosophy (after all, it is the source of both), but it also constitutes the proper measure of their value. The agreement between this language and revelation confirms its rationality, but also the naturalness of revelation, what is more, it undermines the value of any philosophy that contradicts it.

---

25. See: Kaczmarkowski's introduction to the Polish edition of Plato's *Cratylus*, 7–32.

26. Phil. Al., *De opif.* 149–50 [English translation: Philo of Alexandria, *On the Creation of the Cosmos according to Moses*, 86]. See also: Phil. Al., *Leg. alleg.* II.15–18, where he defends the thesis of Adam's authorship of the names given to things against the thesis of the Greek philosophers, which gave priority to the sages.

We shall now return to *The Soul's Testimony*. The analysis of further examples demonstrates their striking convergence with Christian teaching. The spontaneous utterances are treated as an expression of a natural knowledge that is present in the human soul, they confirm the identity of natural knowledge with the many truths revealed by the Creator. This is not only the case with regard to the existence of God. Tertullian says to the soul, "Nor is the nature of the God we declare unknown to thee."[27] Natural reason rejects the indifferent and non-salvific God of the philosophers[28] for the living God of Abraham, Isaac, and Jacob. Against philosophy the soul confirms further truths of Christian teaching: the goodness, omnipotence, omniscience of God, and the anger that all human sin awakens in God; the soul knows of Satan's tricks, it also knows of the last judgment, the possibility of either reward or punishment, or even the truth of the resurrection![29]

How did the soul come to possess this knowledge and what to make of it? These questions pivot upon two words that have played a decisive role in the history of Christian thought: witnessing (*testimonium*) and the witness (*testis*). In these teachings the soul is a witness in a trial of Christian teaching; this witness witnesses about God, but above all, it witnesses about nature—while simultaneously being a part of nature and a representative of nature. We could say that the witness to some degree identifies with what she witnesses for. Tertullian, just like any other enthusiast of teleology, presupposes that coming to know nature is inextricably tied with coming to know its goal and function—it also indirectly means that knowing the nature of the human soul automatically reveals to us some part of God's plans. "These testimonies of the soul are simple as true," says Tertullian, "commonplace as simple, universal as commonplace, natural as universal, divine as natural. I don't think they can appear frivolous or feeble to any one, if he reflects on the majesty of nature, from which the soul derives its authority. If you acknowledge the authority of the mistress, you will own it also in the disciple. Well, nature is the mistress here, and her disciple is the soul. But everything the one has taught or the other learned, has come from God—the Teacher of the teacher."[30] Toward the end of the treatise Tertullian presents a concept that leads the reader to two sources and three witnesses. The witness of the soul is augmented by the witness of the scriptures and those witnesses of the philosophers that were in harmony with the witness of scriptures. These two sources (scripture and nature) ultimately

27. Tert., *Test.* 2, ANF 3, 176.

28. Tertullian takes this up while conducting a polemic against Marcion, a gnostic. See: Tert., *Marc.* II.27.6.

29. See: Tert., *Test.* 3–4.

30. Ibid. 5, ANF 3, 178.

draw from one source; the Bible draws directly from God, whereas philosophy proper draws from nature, which in turn also draws from God: "Believe, then, your own books, and as to our Scriptures so much the more believe writings which are divine, but in the witness of the soul itself give like confidence to Nature. Choose the one of these you observe to be the most faithful friend of truth. If your own writings are distrusted, neither God nor Nature lie."[31]

Upon closer inspection it appears that it becomes increasingly difficult to pigeonhole Tertullian as a thinker who saw revelation as essentially paradoxical, instead Tertullian seems to be closer to seeing revelation as being in accord with the natural knowledge of the soul.[32] However, all of this needs to be nuanced. Everything turns upon evaluating the competence of the soul's testimony. The answer needs to be very much in the spirit of Saint Paul. It seems that these witnesses have a purely theoretical valor, that is, they do not allow one to reach the fullness of perfection. Furthermore, they are incomplete and uncertain (they often contradict each other), especially when one compares them with the revealed truth. Such a judgment about the soul is consistent with Tertullian's attitude toward historical manifestations of philosophy. He considers many of its judgments in harmony with Christian teaching, however, when one takes philosophy in general into consideration then its judgments are so internally contradictory that it is improbable that one would want to use it as a guide toward happiness for the soul. The main value of the soul's testimony lies in its proving the comprehensibility, or at least the non-absurdity of revelation. It can also constitute the starting point for the transformation that can only be fully realized through obedience to Christ. The witness of the soul is not negated, rather, it can only be realized through obedience to Christ. The witness of the soul is not abolished but must be completed by revelation. This is how the soul returns to nature and truly develops. The soul is really naturally Christian, but this only designates a certain orientation of the soul—its natural orientation toward development. In order to become fully perfect it needs to actualize this potential. This is what Tertullian has in mind when he says that the soul is not usually born Christian, but instead becomes Christian.[33] Without the aid of revelation man is exposed to the traps of *hybris*, pride, which misleads reason, and this is most

---

31. Ibid. 6, ANF 3, 179.

32. See: Tert., *Iud.* 2 where the passage from the universal natural law to the law of Moses, and then Christian revelation is understood not as an abolishing, but as an elaboration (by its Author) of the original order, or completion of a work (any change that occurs pertains only to the temporary statutes of the Lawgiver, such as keeping the Sabbath or circumcision). See: *Iud.* 4.1.

33. Tert., *Test.* 1. See: Tert., *An.* 39; Osborn, *The Beginning of Christian Philosophy*, 85.

obvious when we consider the results of pagan philosophy. The example of the philosophers, the students of Greece, teaches us that without revelation the philosopher becomes a collaborator with error. Therefore, the witness of the soul can only constitute a starting point, "But, that we might attain an ampler and more authoritative knowledge at once of himself, and of his counsels and will, God has added a written revelation for the behoof of every one whose heart is set on seeking Him, that seeking he may find, and finding believe, and believing obey."[34]

As we can see, for Tertullian there is contradiction between the statement that Christianity is a philosophy, and that Christianity and Greece are antagonistic realities, and finally, that one of the qualities of truth is its absurdity if it is measured by the corrupt categories of Athens. The portrait of Tertullian as an irrationalist is the effect of identifying philosophy with natural knowledge. But can we really call him a rationalist? We can, but only in a very narrow sense of the word. The portrait of Tertullian as a rationalist should not sidestep the deep sense of God's transcendence in his writings and the absolute peculiarity of "heaven's pupil" who not only should not be, but is not, capable of fully understanding the mysteries of God.

Justin's *Logos*

We are always stuck between two undesirable options whenever we do theology. On the one hand, there is a danger of erasing the difference between revelation and human knowledge. On the other hand, we run the risk of evacuating nature and making revelation totally irrational while making logical and ethical laws hang upon the will of a fickle God. But let us not get sidetracked from the heart of the question. The stance of Justin Martyr is perceived as an example of complete openness toward philosophy which goes so far that it risks the loss of Christian identity. However, the question that constitutes the starting point remains the same: what is the reason behind the existence of elements of authentic (in harmony with revelation) teachings and just living among pagans? While reading Justin we encounter yet another surprise for those who identify philosophy with reason. This is because it appears that Justin (also known as the Philosopher) seems to attribute a much smaller role to natural reason than Tertullian, who is mostly known for his aversion to Athens.

For Justin there seems to be no controversy over the field marked out by the theses in the Epistle to the Romans. The Apologists had no problem

---

34. Tert., *Ap.* 18.1–2, ANF 3, 32.

agreeing about the extent of the most basic knowledge that was made available to people before the advent of revelation (existence of God, his righteousness, the intuition of fundamental moral principles).[35] "[Souls] can perceive that God exists, and that righteousness and piety are honorable,"[36] says Justin. He also adds, in concert with Saint Paul, "it is in the nature of man to know good and evil."[37] According to Justin, this universal ability is the result of participation in the seeds of *logos* (*spermata tou logou*) sowed among men. The question as to how the seeds of the word are related to God's Word and how human reason participates in God's *Logos*, are some of the most contested questions in the research upon Justin's theology.[38]

"We have been taught that Christ is the first-born of God, and we have declared above that He is the Word of whom every race of men were partakers."[39] This is the reason why all those who lived in accord with the gospel, even before the coming of Christ, "are Christians, even though they have been thought atheists."[40] Thanks to "the seed [*sperma*] of reason implanted in every race of men"[41] we can consider Socrates, Heraclitus, Abraham, Ananias, and Elijah believers.[42] Justin does not run the risk of abolishing the difference between philosophy and revelation even though he grants a lot of leeway to Stoics, some poets,[43] and he even considers the teaching of Plato not so much as different from the teaching of Christ, but rather, not quite completely identical with it.[44]

For Justin every philosopher only saw a small portion of the *Logos* germinating within them and was only able to express that small portion of the truth.[45] The philosophers and lawgivers looked into things in a purely human way,[46] but they owed the truth they uncovered to what they partially found

---

35. Pelikan, *The Emergence of the Catholic Tradition*, 32.

36. Iust., *Dial.* 4.7, ANF 1, 197.

37. Iust., *Apol.* II.14.2, ANF 1, 193.

38. My analysis is mainly drawn from the following: Daniélou, *Gospel Message and Hellenistic Culture*, 40–44. See: Holte, "Logos Spermatikos: Christianity and Ancient Philosophy according to Saint Justin Martyr's Apologies," 109–68; Osborn, *The Emergence of Christian Theology*, 268–70.

39. Iust., *Apol.* I.46.2, ANF 1, 178.

40. Ibid. I.46.3, ANF 1, 178.

41. Ibid. II.8.1, ANF 1, 191.

42. Ibid. I.46.3.

43. Ibid. II.7.1.

44. Ibid. II.13.2.

45. Ibid. II.13.3.

46. Ibid. II.10.4.

and saw of the Word.[47] Even though the truths known to philosophers seem to considerably exceed what Saint Paul countenanced in Romans, still Christian teaching, in an obvious way, goes beyond all human learning, "Our doctrines, then, appear to be greater than all human teaching; because Christ, who appeared for our sakes, became the whole rational being, both body, and reason, and soul."[48] The relationship between Christianity and what is authentic in philosophy is analogous to the relationship between the whole and its parts. Whatever is in philosophy is only relative and partial. Whatever does not give full understanding and unshakable knowledge, what causes contradictions in even the most minute matters,[49] becomes the fullness of the Word in Christ. Justin always strongly stressed one very substantial difference: the philosophers never possessed the fullness of the truth. There is a difference between the seed planted by nature, which allows for a very germinal imitation of the Word, as in a mirror darkly, "and quite another is the thing itself, of which there is the participation and imitation according to the grace which is from Him."[50] Christians, "live not according to a part only of the word diffused [among men] but by the knowledge and contemplation of the whole Word, which is Christ."[51]

Famously, according to Harnack, Justin's equating of the *Logos* with Jesus Christ constituted the starting point of Christianity's Hellenization. Yet, for early Christians there was a widespread belief (even present in Tertullian) that the harmony between the laws of nature discovered by reason and God's revealed laws does not cancel out the supernatural, or lead to the naturalization of the Christian truth. Even if the description of the relationship between reason and revelation as the relationship between a part and the whole can seem quite unsatisfactory,[52] it certainly does not undermine the belief in the uniqueness of the Christian claim, nor does it obscure the decisive difference between Christianity and the philosophy of the pagans. If we do not simply identify the approval of natural reason and conscience with an approval of the positive philosophies of the Greeks and Romans, then Harnack's question whether revelation needs rationality[53] can also be put to Saint Paul. And Paul is the concrete inspiration for Justin and the other Apologists when they say

47. Ibid. II.10.2–3.

48. Ibid. II.10.1, ANF 1, 191.

49. Ibid. II.13.3, II.10.3.

50. Ibid. II.13.5, ANF 1, 193.

51. Ibid. II.8.3, ANF 1, 191.

52. See: Armstrong and Markus, *Christian Faith and Greek Philosophy*, 170.

53. Adolf Harnack, *History of Dogma*, 100–101.

that revelation is above reason, but does not contradict it. If that is not the case then revelation would abolish nature, and then nobody could possibly judge the morality and relevance of anything that remains outside of Christ. The need for revelation was obvious (or, as I will argue, decisive) even for enthusiasts of Greek thought like Justin, yet, there were serious disagreements about how much wisdom and virtue could be found in pagan wisdom. This is because for the fathers rationality, in the strictest sense of the word, requires faith: "But pray that, above all things, the gates of light may be opened to you; for these things cannot be perceived or understood by all, but only by the man to whom God and His Christ have imparted wisdom."[54]

This brings up a whole series of questions. Is natural reason the sole source of truth whose resonances in Stoic ethics and Platonic theology are a cause of wonderment for us? Or, is it thanks to the seeds of reason within human nature that Socrates and Heraclitus could be Christians before Christ? Is it true that the identification of the *Logos* with Christ really permits Justin to gesture toward a life in accord with revealed teaching as the ultimate realization of the philosophical ideal of a life lived in accord with reason? First of all, when Justin identifies the *Logos* with Jesus he does not say that Christ-*Logos* and the seeds of the *logos* dispersed throughout nature are wholly identical. We can assume that Justin is talking about two different *logoi*, that of Christ (the *Logos*) and that of reason (*spermata tou logou*). If the second *logos* is the gift of a basic knowledge, given to all people by God, and thanks to its universality acknowledged as natural, then participation in the first *logos* is a kind of special pre-Christian revelation, which only pertains to very few sages such as Socrates or Heraclitus (and in turn explains the unusual depth of their intuition and the perfection of their lives, even if their knowledge of the Word before the incarnation was only partial). It is only when we analyze the relationship between the scattered seeds of the *logos* and the *Logos* of Christ that we can answer the question whether, as Eusebius put it, Justin wearing the cape of a philosopher proclaimed the Word of God,[55] or, as Harnack would have it, Justin was philosophical to the core and there was not even a scrap of theology in him. We must be very careful in our analysis of the analogies so that we do not end up saying something Justin did not say. Justin did indeed clearly say that "He is the Word of whom every race of men were partakers."[56] What is more, "on account of the seed of reason [the *Logos*] implanted in every

---

54. Iust., *Dial.* VII.3, ANF 1, 198.

55. Eus., *HE* IV.11.8.

56. Iust., *Apol.* I.46.2, ANF 1, 178.

race of men"[57] the Christ "is diffused among men."[58] Justin even goes as far as saying that the ability for moral discernment that originates in the *Logos* is part of the nature of humanity[59] and that the seeds of the *logos* are in humans thanks to nature putting them there.[60] The *Logos* is related to the *logos*-reason just as the whole is related to the part, which greatly complicates the transcendence of the *Logos*, but it does elevate the significance of reason.[61]

If, however, we accept that the *Logos* that inspired Socrates and Heraclitus remains transcendent to nature, then we must admit that Justin concedes much less to natural reason than, for example, Tertullian. The wisdom of the pagans so admired by Justin, only revealed to the select, is a revelation that is incomplete, but still supernatural, just like the revelation of Christ.[62] If that is the case then there can be no talk of affirming the natural possibilities of reason. Reason not inspired by the *Logos* is not capable of more than an intuition of God's existence and a jumble of the most basic moral tenets. Once more, although from a different perspective, we can see that the early Christian attitudes toward ancient philosophers cannot be applied to their evaluations of natural reason.[63] In the instance of Justin this can be untangled by considering

57. Ibid. II.7.1, ANF 1, 191.

58. Ibid. II.7.3, ANF 1, 191.

59. Ibid. II.14.2.

60. Ibid. II.13.5–6.

61. Henry Chadwick observes that for Justin—who combined the distinction between the Father and the Son with the Platonic distinction between God in himself and God in relation to the world—the Father signifies the transcendent God, while the Son signifies the immanent God [*Philo and the Beginning of Christian Thought*, 163]. As Daniélou notes, while reading Justin, we are obviously dealing with a contrast between the transcendent and invisible Father and the Son who is understood as the instrument of God's activity in the world (*Gospel Message and Hellenistic Culture*, 345). J. N. D. Kelly rightfully alerts us to the dangers inherent in applying later post-Nicean conceptions, especially the fully developed doctrine of hypostases, to the Apologists (*Early Christian Doctrines*, 101–3). This is why it makes more sense to side with Osborn when he says, "the nature of the Logos is both exalted, transcendent, omnipresent, and immanent." Eric Osborn, *Justin Martyr*, 35.

62. This confirms Justin's understanding of philosophy as a gift (*Dial.*, II.1–2).

63. When answering the question of the origins of Greek wisdom, Clement of Alexandria makes a distinction between the natural reason available to all human beings (*koinos nous*), which only gives access to the most elementary knowledge about God, and inspiration (*proanafonesis, sinekfonesis*), given to the chosen (*Str.* I.XVI.80.5; LXVIII.94.1–4; VI.VII.55.4; VI.XVII.158, 1–2). For example, among the Greeks Homer, Pythagoras, and Plato (ibid. V.V.29.4; V.XIV.116.1; VI.XVII.154.4) had it, although Clement does not limit it to the Greeks only (ibid. I.XV.71.3). It is obvious how much this distinction diminishes natural reason, which might seem shocking in a thinker who is generally considered to be a great friend of pagan philosophy. It is yet another

the relation of the seed-*logos* and the *Logos* of Christ in his writings.[64] If a radical discontinuity reigns there, then Tertullian with his witness of the soul goes much further than Justin toward Christian rationalism. This rationalism finds its ultimate expression in the writings of Anselm of Canterbury, who considers it possible to prove nearly all Christian dogmas through natural reason.

I do not want to discuss Anselm's position here. What I have said should only serve as a warning against the urge to attribute to the Apologists positions that are not found in their texts, that is, the medieval definition of the relationship of faith to reason. It cannot be found in either Justin or Tertullian, but it also cannot be found in Paul, and, after all, the Epistle to the Romans is one of the core texts of Christianity. Looking at things from the perspective that was most important for the ancients, that is from the perspective of effects, natural knowledge is related to knowledge through faith just as uncertain knowledge, often contradictory and partial, is related to full and true knowledge. When we remember that both faith and reason are supposed to serve the attainment of perfection, then the superiority of faith seems obvious.

In agreement with the tradition of Jewish Hellenism, many Christians will admit that natural knowledge is weighed down by the fact that it is not direct knowledge.[65] Even if, as the apostle says, creation makes visible the invisible attributes of God, it is still burdened with all the defects and dangers inherent in making judgments about the original while only having access to its shadow. The different areas of reach are explained by the different object of direct knowledge. Knowledge of God mediated through the knowledge of the senses inevitably marks the knowledge gained through this approach with the defective properties of sublunar reality. The world weighs down the knowledge of God gained through its mediation with its own mutability, that is, uncertainty and impermanence.[66] From this point of view religious knowledge is

---

proof that respect for philosophy did not go hand in hand with acknowledging wide possibilities for reason. Philosophy is mainly understood as a gift analogical to the Law given to the chosen people (ibid. VI.VI.44.1; VII.II.10.2–11). Both in Clement's and Justin's eyes, the splendor of philosophy (much like the Law) comes from it being merely one part of the divine economy of salvation, rather than the triumphal history of reason (ibid. I.V.28.1–3; VI.V.42.3). Clement even goes as far as calling philosophy a testament (*diatheke*) (ibid. VI.VIII.67.1). With regard to this matter: Daniélou, *Gospel Message and Hellenistic Culture*, 48–73. Daniélou emphasizes how especially pessimistic Clement was about the abilities of unaided reason and how much his attacks owed to the skeptics who loved to point out the contradictions and disagreements between philosophers (70). See: Osborn, *The Philosophy of Clement of Alexandria*, 123.

64. See: Osborn, *The Beginning of Christian Philosophy*, 80.

65. Phil. Al., *Leg. alleg.* III.99–100.

66. Ibid. III.101.

not only fuller, but also more certain. Even if faith rooted in revelation (in its certainty, immutability, and reach) later makes way for direct knowledge face to face, its sources lie in an act of unmediated knowledge, an act described with metaphors such as "seeing" or "touching" God. Yet, these are the summits that can be only reached by way of a long journey during which reason and faith must support each other mutually.

The complementarity of faith and reason is already inscribed into the Pauline formulation of a possibility of knowing God in his works. The knowledge that is given through the mediation of revelation and natural knowledge possesses different degrees of certainty, different sources, and different reaches, but they are both indubitably in accordance with reason. Independently of how far the earthly ladder can take reason within its purely natural boundaries, this ladder is most certainly propped against the gates of heaven, therefore it is also the same ladder revealed truth uses to descend toward the earth. The propositions of the Apologists, which stress the transcendence of God and the final goal of humanity, point toward a considerable convergence between nature and revelation. Even though Christians obviously modified the Greek concepts of nature and reason, that is, they were well acquainted with the difference between the God of the Christians and the God of the philosophers (as Tertullian put it), they did not create some totally new rationality that "tear[s] out from our being all the postulates of our 'natural knowledge' and our 'natural morality.'"[67] Here the goal of humanity lies beyond the nature that can be comprehended by reason and as such it is in some way unknowable. That is to say, humanity is not capable of fully understanding the paradoxical rules of Christian life revealed by Christ. However, human nature can only fully realize itself by striving toward this goal, which is given in a life ordered toward God and in accord with revealed principles. Sanctity is a perfection of those who are absorbed in a transcendence that goes beyond reason and nature. For all the differences between the several possible articulations of this position, this much is always in accord. And yet reason is not an asylum for people who are dispirited and overawed by revealed mysteries, instead, it is a talent that should not be buried. The reply to mystery should be humility caused by the consciousness of the limits of one's reason, rather than an escape into rationalism.

Paradoxically—and surprisingly enough this is probably most important to Tertullian among all early Christian thinkers—the Christianity of fideists, a Christianity that proudly turns the other cheek after the beating it has received from haughty reason, is a deeply pitiful sight.

---

67. Lev Shestov, *Athens and Jerusalem*, 288.

3

How Much Wisdom Is There in Philosophy?

Doctrinal Similarities

THE COMPLEMENTARITY OF REASON and revelation need not always go hand in hand with an agreement between revelation and already existing philosophies. This is because philosophy is not always the rightful heir of reason. Yet, "not always" does not mean "never." We know with all certainty that already at the turn of the second century CE there were anthologies that collected those fragments of outstanding pagan writers presentable as being in tune with Christian teaching:

> Indeed, some of our people, who still continued their inquisitive labors in ancient literature, and still occupied memory with it, have published works we have in our hands of this very sort; works in which they relate and attest the nature and origin of their traditions, and the grounds on which opinions rest, and from which it may be seen at once that we have embraced nothing new or monstrous—nothing for which we cannot claim the support of ordinary and well-known writings, whether in ejecting error from our creed, or admitting truth into it.[1]

Independently of how this fact was interpreted and used, nobody denied that the ancient teachings contained seeds of truth, and even for Tertullian the whole history of philosophy could not be reduced to merely "Greece" plus "Athens" equaling "the love of error." Here we will attempt to outline the

---

1. Tert., *Test.* 1, ANF 3, 174.

accepted reach of the similarities while leaving the discussion of how these writings were used for chapter 4 of this book.

In our search for a reconstruction of the works mentioned by Tertullian we can find help in Christian apologies that frequently featured separate chapters devoted to this problem.[2] They followed certain general principles—even if the evaluations of individual writers frequently demonstrate the presence of individual preferences—about the intellectual formation in particular pagan philosophical contexts, plus a varied range of enthusiasm about discovering the existence of such overlaps. The greatest attention was paid to those writings that stressed final causes which prove the existence of the one, immaterial, and transcendent God. The least attention was given to the mechanists, atheists, materialists, fatalists, and those who deprecated the rule of God's providence over the world. These are the reasons why Plato was so popular, especially the *Timaeus* (its demiurge), *Gorgias* (the judgment of the soul), or the *Seventh Letter* (the inexpressibility of knowledge about God). It was also the reason why the Stoics garnered so much respect, especially because of their strict ideals about living properly. On the other hand, there was a universal rejection of the Atomists and Epicureans, because they did not subscribe to these principles. The intellectual tendencies of each writer account for the wide distribution of sympathies, and whether differences or similarities with Christian doctrine were stressed. As we recall, for these early Christian thinkers the teaching of Plato is considerably different from Christianity despite its similarities, whereas Socrates is a Christian who lived before Christ. On the other hand, even though Tertullian was full of doubts with regard to Socrates,[3] he thought that the Roman Stoic Seneca was "often ours" (*saepe noster*).[4] The philosophical ear of every individual Christian writer is the other factor (besides individual philosophical preferences) that determines the range of acceptable similarities. Tertullian sharply saw how it would be very difficult to square the immutable God of the philosophers (a God who does not offer much ground for hope) with the God of revelation. The critical mind of Tertullian did not ignore the difficulties standing in the way of all attempts at reconciling faith in God's wrath with the immutable and dispassionate being of the First Cause.[5]

---

2. See: Min. Fel., *Oct.* 19.3–15; Clem. Al., *Protr.* 6.67—7.76.

3. Tert., *Ap.* 14.7; 21.1–2; 39.12–13; *Nat.* I.4. Adolf Harnack wrote about the relationship of the fathers of the church to Socrates in his classic study "Sokrates und die Alte Kirche" [Socrates and the Old Church], 24–48. See also: Thomas Deman, *Chrystus Pan i Sokrates* [Christ the Lord and Socrates] (No English translation is available —trans.)

4. Tert., *An.* 20.1. On Tertullian's relationship with Stoicism see the following: Colisch, *The Stoic Tradition from Antiquity to the Early Middle Ages*, 13–29.

5. See: Tert., *Test.* 2.

Yet, this does not mean that the God of the philosophers is the God of reason. On the contrary! For Tertullian, the testimony of the soul—the Stoic *sensus communis,* in other words, reasonable knowledge—demonstrates the *unreasonableness* of philosophical theses. Yet, this problem does not seem to trouble Justin Martyr at all.

The range of approved similarities also depends upon the willingness of the theologian to allegorically interpret the conclusions of philosophy. The allegorical method, which originated in the Alexandrian tradition, allows the interpreter to treat some of the philosophical texts as Christian texts encoded out of fear of exposing them to those who might profane them, or, to those who are the enemies of the truth.[6] The roots of this hermeneutic method can be found in the allegorical interpretation of the mythologies found in Homer and Hesiod that were scoured for their hidden symbols, for example, either cosmological or ethical symbols (one instance of this is the work of the Stoic Corinthus). Philo of Alexandria played a seminal role in the development of this method as a tool for mediating between philosophy and revelation. For example, there is his commentary on the Pentateuch where he finds, among other things, a symbolic rendition of Stoic virtue. The allegorical method, which was primarily used to uncover the deeper spiritual sense of the scriptures, was also utilized as a way of adopting pagan philosophy for theology. Minucius Felix serves as a good Christian example. He saw the teaching of Thales on water as the ultimate *archē* as being analogous to the sacrament of baptism.[7] We can console those who only see arbitrariness in allegory by pointing out how thanks to it we still have many pagan texts that otherwise would have been lost in the mists of time, because they would have been considered unintelligent, scandalous, or damaging.

Philosophy as a Guide to Life

Despite these many differences we can formulate a second principle, even if it is also burdened with exceptions. We must conclude there was a greater tendency to acknowledge the reasonableness of certain philosophical statements,

---

6. Clement gives a thorough explanation of the allegorical and symbolic methods, all the while stressing the apophatic character of revelation itself (*Str.* VI.XV.126.1–4). On allegory in Greek, Jewish, and Christian thought see: Zieliński, *Jerozolimy, Ateny, Aleksandria* [Jerusalem, Athens, Alexandria], 94–145. Also see the chapter entitled "Symbolism" in Osborn, *The Philosophy of Clement of Alexandria,* 168–74.

7. Min. Fel., *Oct.* 19.4. We should also mention that the allegorical interpretation leads not only to uncovering religious elements of philosophy, but also the philosophical elements in the Bible.

than to acknowledge that all philosophers were sages (meaning, that they lived in full accordance with reason).[8] With the exception of Justin, and even he had some reservations, Christians were unwilling to give their approval to philosophy's similarities to revelation when faced with arguments that individual philosophers lived lives of perfection. The perfection of individual philosophers brings the issue to a head and ultimately allows for the most clear judgment of how much of ancient philosophy can be embraced by Christians. The most properly framed question does not attempt to determine whether there are accidental overlaps between philosophy and revelation, and it does not attempt to discover whether there is something reasonable in philosophy. Instead, the real question is as follows: is there enough truth in philosophy to guide one's life according to its lights in order to live a life in accord with reason? That is, even if one cannot live a perfectly Christian life (impossible without revelation anyway), then can one at least live reasonably by following positive philosophy?

Tatian the Syrian is an example of a negative answer to this question. The heart of the matter for him is not in one's opinion about the possibility of coming to know the truth, instead it is found in how philosophers were able to utilize that truth. His writings confirm our earlier distinction between being anti-philosophical and anti-rational. Tatian unswervingly admits that men possess the ability to know God naturally through his creatures[9] and affirms a life lived in accord with reason.[10] He also accepts as obvious the convergence of many philosophical truths and Christianity. However, even if this is what encouraged Saint Justin to look upon philosophy favorably, it became for his student, Tatian, the basis for polemics against philosophy. After all, why should we admire those who did not take advantage of the opportunity to read the book of nature granted to them by God? Why should we admire thieves who not only stole[11] whatever was valuable in the concept of nature, but also destroyed the concept of nature by peppering it with lies, contradictions, and errors? Even though there are many traces of the truth (not everything was spoiled) in philosophy it would be very difficult to find examples of lives that

8. Domański, "Metamorfozy pojecia filozofii," 21.

9. Tatian writes: "Him we know from His creation, and apprehend His invisible power by His works." Tat., *Or.* 4, ANF 2, 66.

10. That a life lived in accord with reason is a life lived in accord with the will of God is apparent, for example, when he says that demons deceived humanity by saying that even the most irrational earthly life could be in accord with reason if lived in harmony with the stars. See: Tat., *Or.* 9.

11. Ibid. 1.35–40. See: Iust., *Apol.* I.44.8–10; I.44.59–60. Min. Fel. *Oct.* 20.1; 34.5. Tert., *Ap.* 19.

could be admired by Christians without reservation, or, admired at all. Here is a sample of Tatian's style: "What noble thing have you produced by your pursuit of philosophy? Who of your most eminent men has been free from vain boasting? Diogenes, who made such a parade of his independence with his tub, was seized with a bowel complaint through eating a raw polypus, and so lost his life by gluttony. Aristippus, walking about in a purple robe, led a profligate life, in accordance with his professed opinions. Plato, a philosopher, was sold by Dionysius for his gormandizing propensities. And Aristotle, who absurdly placed a limit to Providence and made happiness to consist in the things which give pleasure, quite contrary to his duty as a preceptor flattered Alexander, forgetful that he was but a youth; and he, showing how well he had learned the lessons of his master, because his friend would not worship him, shut him up and carried him about like a bear or a leopard."[12]

Tatian's opinions do not substantially swerve from mainline views about this matter, even though not all the Christian writers were equally fanatical and unconditional. Tertullian, who probably would have made an exception for Seneca, would in principle agree with Tatian. The philosophers had access to the truth, but they did not use the counsels of nature, nor what they had learned from Moses. "Therefore he who shall have the fear of God," says Tertullian, "even if he be ignorant of all things else, if he has attained to the knowledge and truth of God, will possess full and perfect wisdom."[13] But this does not pertain to the philosophers who generally prefer to believe in falsehoods rather than the truth.[14] The witness of their writings shows that they knew the truth at least partially. That they decapitated, maimed, and mixed the truth with falsehoods is witnessed by the numerous contradictions in their teachings and the general wickedness of pagan life. The cause of the errors is

---

12. Tat., *Or.* 2, ANF 2, 65. Here I am developing an argument I began in my earlier book *Arcyparadoks smierci* [*The Archparadox of Death*], 141–42. When we read the Apologists we should remember the Christians do not have a monopoly on deriding the philosophers and their lives. This harsh style of writing even earned itself the name (derived from the cynical philosopher Menippos) of Menippean satire. Whoever has read the satires of Lucian knows the severity of his judgments do not take a back seat to Tatian: pointing out the disharmony between teaching and life is crucial for him. For example, "Everything they preach—how they scorn money and fame, consider beauty the only good, are above anger, look down their noses at celebrities and address them as equals—god knows is fine and wise and wonderful, very much and truly so. But they teach these very things for pay! They worship wealth, their mouths water for money, these creatures who are more snappish than curs, more timid than rabbits, more fawning than monkeys, more thieving than weasels, more lascivious than jackasses, more quarrelsome than cocks" from Lucian, *Pisc.* 34, 351–52.

13. Tert., *Nat.* II.2, ANF 3, 130.

14. See: Tert., *Test.* 1.

twofold: the lust for knowledge and the lust for fame.[15] The problem does not only stem from the fact that the philosophers overlooked, misunderstood, or disbelieved in everything they took from the Scriptures. "The consequence of this is," says Tertullian, "that even that which [the philosophers] had discovered degenerated into uncertainty, and there arose from one or two drops of truth a perfect flood of argumentation."[16] It seems philosophy is unsure and wavering, therefore it follows from this that philosophy is completely useless as a guide for life. There are no traces of perfection in it, furthermore, what passes as perfection is merely the by-product of the lust for fame, instead of being a proof of possessing the truth, and the strength of a mind liberated from the lower passions. This is the true face of the famed exploits of Empedocles, Anaxarchus, Xeno, Regulus, all whom Tertullian lists as being equal in courage with the Athenian Leaena.[17] The perfections of Heraclitus or Peregrinus are also only too apparent.[18] Tertullian does not waver in questioning the wisdom of Socrates, not only because some of his views are patent absurdities,[19] but also because his actions reveal more hubris than one could expect from a rationality derived from knowledge of the truth.[20]

Philosophy's Irrationalities and Contradictions

The Apologists had two main reasons for rejecting philosophy as a way of life, meaning, as an alternative on equal footing with Christianity. The first is connected to how various philosophical viewpoints contradicted each other.

---

15. See: Tert. *Ap.* 46.7.

16. Tert., *Nat.* II.2, ANF 3, 130. Clement of Alexandria supports Tertullian's position when he says, "Since, therefore, truth is one (for falsehood has ten thousand by-paths); just as the Bacchantes tore asunder the limbs of Pentheus, so the sects both of barbarian and Hellenic philosophy have done with truth, and each vaunts as the whole truth the portion which has fallen to its lot." Clem. Al., *Str.* I.XIII.57.1, ANF 2, 313. A similar view of philosophy's interminable divisions came to life much later from the pen of Boethius of Dacia.

17. See: Tert., *Ap.* 50.4–9.

18. See: Tert., *Mart.* 4.

19. Tert., *Nat.* I.4. Here Tertullian is particularly concerned with the problem of placing demons above God. See: Tert., *Ap.*, 14.7; 22.1–2. See: Stępień, "Ojcowie Koscioła i demon Sokratesa" [Fathers of the Church and the Daimonion of Socrates], 242–51.

20. The episode in *The Republic* (457c–d) where Socrates puts forward his theses about polygamy are used as a proof of Socrates's immorality and are treated by Tertullian as a form of prostitution (see: *Ap.* 39.12–13). Tertullian is also willing to seriously consider the Athenian accusations of corrupting the youth (See: *Ap.* 46.10).

The second is connected to obvious falsehood. The contradictions led to uncertainty, while falsehoods led to immorality.[21]

Let us begin with the notion of falsehood. Even though philosophy has many overlaps with Christian teaching, it also abounds in many conclusions not compatible with Christianity. The following topics are especially glaring areas of doctrinal difference: the doctrine of God, the soul, human nature, and ultimate happiness. The differences with the mechanists are glaring enough to not warrant a discussion; instead we shall concentrate upon a critique of false classical Greek theology. This argument derives from the belief that only true knowledge of the Author of reality, and attuning one's life to his decrees, will lead to a life of perfection. This is closely connected to the presupposition about the close affinity between the best part of the human soul and God. A correct identification of God is then connected with the identification of what is best in humanity. Furthermore, only a life lived in accord with the best part of ourselves, a life that actualizes the most godlike part of ourselves, will lead to perfection. This manner of thinking, perfectly understandable to the Greeks, is also accepted by Tatian (based upon Genesis 1:26), who maintains that humanity is not only a rational animal, but also the image and likeness of God: "Man is not, as the croaking philosophers say, merely a rational animal capable of understanding and knowledge; for, according to them, even irrational creatures appear possessed of understanding and knowledge. But man alone is the image and likeness of God; and I mean by man, not one who performs actions similar to those of animals, but one who has advanced far beyond mere humanity—to God Himself."[22]

We should understand this statement in light of Plato's definition of philosophy as the work of divinization.[23] When we take physical matter to be the god and principle of this world, then materialism will direct our lives and the passions will be acknowledged as the highest part of our nature. This way of thinking clearly applies not only to matter, but also to everything else that is lower than the true God. This is what Tatian had in mind writing about reducing the human to the animal, that is, reducing the reasonable to something lacking reason. The quality of one's conversion will depend upon the ultimate principle ruling it: "Such is the nature of man's constitution; and, if it be like

21. Here he seems to be relying upon Irenaeus's distinction between the godless and sinners. The godless are those who do not know God and do not worship him, whereas the sinners are those who know God, but do not follow his commands, instead they flout them. See: Iren., *Demonstr.* 2.

22. Tat., *Or.* 15, ANF 2, 71.

23. There is an exhaustive discussion of philosophy understood as divinization in my book *Arcyparadoks śmierci* [*The Archparadox of Death*], 205–37.

a temple, God is pleased to dwell in it by the spirit, His representative; but, if it be not such a habitation, man excels the wild beasts in articulate language only; in other respects his manner of life is like theirs, as one who is not a likeness of God."[24] This manner of thinking already appeared in full force in Paul's Epistle to the Romans. Idolatry and immorality are the effect of accepting a false image of reality; it is the flip-side of a unified phenomenon. When we elevate something lower than God to the rank of the highest principle, then we simultaneously commit an act of idolatry and submit our lives to a principle that reduces our humanity to submission to its lower elements. "While claiming to be wise, they became fools and exchanged the glory of the immortal God for the likeness of an image of mortal man or of birds or of four-legged animals or of snakes. Therefore, God handed them over to impurity through the lusts of their hearts for the mutual degradation of their bodies. They exchanged the truth of God for a lie and revered and worshiped the creature rather than the creator, who is blessed forever. Amen. Therefore, God handed them over to degrading passions" (Rom 1:22–26). Paul's opinion is pithily compressed by Chesterton's ironic claim that when people stop believing in God they will not stop believing, rather, they will believe anything. We should note how in this statement knowledge and virtue are closely tied, much as they are for the majority of ancient philosophers and writers. Whoever does not know God, and glorifies a false god-principle, cannot live a virtuous life. When God is not the structuring principle of our knowledge, when there is no God behind our judgments, then the religious name for this state of life is idolatry, while its moral effect is immorality.

Therefore, there is nothing unusual about Christians using this theme to critique both pagan religion and philosophy. "Now, then, clear out all the thoughts that take up your attention, and pack away all the old ways of looking at things that keep deceiving you. You must become like a new man from the beginning, since, as you yourself admit, you are going to listen to a really new message. Look at the things that you proclaim and think of as gods. See with your outward eyes and with your mind what material they are made of and what form they happen to have."[25] This statement is not only addressed against the gods of pagan religion, but also against the philosophical principles of reality. This is because all of the following practices name a phenomenon other than God as their ultimate principle: the barbarian cult of worshiping

24. Tat., *Or.* 15, ANF 2, 71.
25. *Ad Diog.* 2.1, ANF 1, 214.

natural phenomena,²⁶ oriental mysteries,²⁷ the immorality of poetic and mythological Olympians,²⁸ the cult of statues (made by human hands),²⁹ philosophico-religious speculations about stellar intelligences, or the *archai* of the philosophers.³⁰ The highest principle (*archē*) was always divine for the Greeks.

---

26. See: Arist., *Apol.* 3, ANF 9, 265. There Aristides argues the following: "The Barbarians, then, as they did not apprehend God, went astray among the elements, and began to worship things created instead of their Creator; and for this end they made images and shut them up in shrines, and lo! they worship them, guarding them the while with much care, lest their gods be stolen by robbers. And the Barbarians did not observe that that which acts as guard is greater than that which is guarded, and that everyone who creates is greater than that which is created. If it be, then, that their gods are too feeble to see to their own safety, how will they take thought for the safety of men? Great then is the error into which the Barbarians wandered in worshiping lifeless images which can do nothing to help them. And I am led to wonder, O King, at their philosophers, how that even they went astray, and gave the name of gods to images which were made in honor of the elements; and that their sages did not perceive that the elements also are dissoluble and perishable."

27. Clement of Alexandria, toward the end of a document concerned with the mysteries writes, "Such are the mysteries of the Atheists. And with reason I call those Atheists who know not the true God, and pay shameless worship to a boy torn in pieces by the Titans, and a woman in distress, and to parts of the body that in truth cannot be mentioned for shame, held fast as they are in the double impiety, first in that they know not God, not acknowledging as God Him who truly is; the other and second is the error of regarding those who exist not, as existing and calling those gods that have no real existence, or rather no existence at all, who have nothing but a name." Clem. Al., *Protr.* 2.23.1., ANF 2, 177.

28. "The Greeks, then, because they are more subtle than the Barbarians, have gone further astray than the Barbarians; inasmuch as they have introduced many fictitious gods, and have set up some of them as males and some as females; and in that some of their gods were found who were adulterers, and did murder, and were deluded, and envious, and wrathful and passionate, and parricides, and thieves, and robbers. . . . Thus, O King, have the Greeks put forward foulness, and absurdity, and folly about their gods and about themselves, in that they have called those that are of such a nature gods, who are no gods. And hence mankind have received incitements to commit adultery and fornication, and to steal and to practice all that is offensive and hated and abhorred. For if they who are called their gods practiced all these things which are written above, how much more should men practice them—men, who believe that their gods themselves practiced them." Arist., *Apol.* 8, ANF 9, 269. See: Clem. Al., *Protr.* 4.46–63; Min. Fel., *Oct.* 23.1–13.

29. See: *Ad Diog.* 2.1–10; Min. Fel., *Oct.* 24.5–8.

30. "Let us then run over, if you choose, the opinions of the philosophers, to which they give boastful utterance, respecting the gods; that we may discover philosophy itself, through its conceit making an idol of matter," writes Clement of Alexandria while discussing the doctrines of Thales, Anaximenes, Diogenes, Parmenides, Heraclitus, and Empedocles. He strove to mention just about every philosopher, so that their errors would not be passed over in silence. See: Clem. Al., *Protr.* 5.64–66, ANF 2, 190.

This tendency was at the root of the popular Christian theory that it was the demons, fallen angels, who were the authors of false philosophy and religion. The demons are lower than God, bound to matter, and the object and cause of false worship, which dehumanizes humanity.[31] We should not forget that the Christian theologians utilized many arguments lifted out of the Greeks, but against the Greeks. The critique of the anthropomorphism and immorality of polytheistic religion was—at least since the time of Xenophanes—a basic weapon in the Greek philosophical armory. The Christians borrowed weapons from this armory at will. It is enough to mention how three important fragments of Xenophanes survived only because they were so popular among Christians.[32] The theory of Euhemerus of Messene, arguing that the gods were merely divinized humans, was also extremely popular.[33] The Christians willingly used the heritage of the Greek poets, philosophers, and orators whenever it was useful to them. If anyone is offended by the lack of good will and superficial judgments of the Christian writers, let him reach for the works of, say, Lucian and he will realize how the pamphlets of he Apologists do not stray from the then-accepted tone of religious polemics. The only novelty of the Christian works lies in their awareness that the things they are discussing are a matter of life and death, even more, of eternal life and eternal death. This is obviously why the debt to the Greeks is not only a matter of form. It is enough to peek into Tertullian's works to see with what ease the concepts of eternity, movement, permanence, or of the Prime Mover are put to work in criticizing pagan religion.[34] It would be difficult to deny that the Christian effort to undermine Greek theology was accomplished through recycling Greece's very highest intellectual achievements.

If falsehood leads directly to immorality then the contradictions discoverable upon comparing the positions of different philosophers prove that their theses are burdened by a lack of certainty and as such they cannot play the role of a solid foundation for spiritual transformation, "You mean of course, that pure and simple wisdom of the philosophers which attests its own weakness mainly by that variety of opinion which proceeds from an ignorance of the truth."[35] The widely discussed notion of the internal inconsistency of philosophy equally originated in the confrontation of particular doctrines with the

31. This factor was also usually combined with the cult of stellar intelligences. See: Tat., *Or.* 7, 9; Min. Fel., *Oct.* 26.8; Tert., *Ap.* 22; Iust., *Apol.* I.5.2.

32. Clem. Al., *Str.* V.XIV.109.1–3; VII.VII.22.1. See: Osborn, *Irenaeus of Lyons*, 157.

33. Tertullian devoted the whole second part of *To the Nations* (especially *Nat.* II.3–6) to this topic.

34. Tert., *Nat.* II.2, ANF 3, 130.

35. Ibid.

expectations of Christians and the comparison of stances taken up in the most important controversies of ancient philosophy. For the Christians individual philosophers contradict themselves whenever they affirm certain truths thought to be Christian while they contradict others. However, in Christian writings, the theme of contradiction sprouted mainly out of the disagreements among opinions held by various philosophical schools. "For all these, having fallen in love with vain and empty reputation, neither themselves knew the truth, nor guided others to the truth: for the things which they said themselves convict them of speaking inconsistently; and most of them demolished their own doctrines. For not only did they refute one another, but some, too, even stultified their own teachings; so that their reputation has issued in shame and folly, for they are condemned by men of understanding."[36] The Christians were not direct participants of these debates, as outsiders they were content to observe the inescapable differences between philosophers. They were succored by a long line of skeptical philosophy, which since the times of Timon of Philus collected these divergences as an indirect proof of the inconclusiveness of the issues raised by the dogmatic philosophers. They were examples of isosthenia, that is, of the equal power of contradictory philosophical judgments.[37]

"[The] philosophers put forth their doctrines, saying things that neither sound the same, nor mean the same as one another."[38] The Christians were more than willing to expose this discord. Hermias, who wrote sometime near the end of the second century devoted a whole treatise to it. In his *Derision of Gentile Philosophers* Hermias presents the differences that divide the philosophers on questions as basic to our lives as happiness, the nature of the soul, reason, the ultimate principle, and even the concept of God. "What then must we term these things? They seem to me, to be a prodigy, or folly, or madness, or rebellion, or all these together."[39] I will not attempt to sort out how much Hermias owes his stylistic verve to Timon, but there is no doubt that he uses this style for an entirely different purpose, that is, to demonstrate the soundness of Christianity and the uselessness of philosophy as a sufficient guide toward perfection. "These things have I gone through," writes Hermias

---

36. Theo., *Ad Autol.* 3.3, ANF 2, 111.

37. Cicero, in his *On Academic Skepticism*, gives a comical picture of the irresolvable controversies between various philosophical schools—only the skeptics came out on top. The Christians probably willingly took in the skeptical critique of the Dogmatic school. It is telling that this particular fragment from Cicero came down to us through Saint Augustine, who cited it in its entirety and only critiqued its conclusion in favor of the skeptics. See: Augustinus, *Contra Accademicos* III.7.15–16.

38. Herm., *Irr.* 1 in: *The Writings of the Early Christians of the Second Century*, 193.

39. Ibid. 2, 194.

in the last sentence of his work, "wishing to point out the opposition which is in their doctrines, and how their examination of things will go on to infinity and no limit, for their end is inexplicable and useless, being confirmed neither by one manifest fact, nor by one sound argument."[40] The lack of agreement proves philosophy's lack of grounding, whereas its lack of certainty suggests its uselessness.

It really might seem like Justin stands on the other side of the barricades from the perspective of Tatian, Hermias, or Tertullian. This is because he not only tries to prove doctrinal similarities, but, it also *seems*, he argues for such a wide range of these similarities because, in principle, they allow for the attainment of Christian perfection before the coming of Christ. The issue at hand is extremely important, because philosophy, above all, as we have already argued, is a way of life in competition with Christianity; it is a method whose aim is to reach happiness understood as the state proper to the perfection of human nature. And yet Justin's position, upon closer inspection, is not an exception in this case. His affirmation of the lives lived in perfection—those of Socrates or Heraclitus for example—is qualified by reservations, which leave no doubts about Justin's most important commitments.

The philosophers, because they did not know the fullness of the Word, often contradicted each other.[41] While these contradictions were proof that, "on the more important points [the philosophers] appear not to have possessed the heavenly wisdom, and the knowledge which cannot be spoken against."[42]

Let us stop here. This is an important statement for understanding Justin. It means that Socrates, through living in accordance with the *logos*, lived a perfect life, but the foundation of his decision was not certain and properly understood truth, instead it was an uncertain opinion. In the language of ancient philosophy this does mean that Socrates was a sage, but only by chance, because he reached his natural perfection through a happy convergence of coincidences, blind chance, or, and this is probably what Justin hoped, through freely given grace without regard for human merits. This is not a compliment the Greek philosopher might have anticipated or accepted. Such a judgment clearly discredits the philosophy of Socrates, if we are to understand it as a path toward an authentic human life. It places his philosophy on the side of matters worthy of attention, rather than those worthy of imitation.[43]

---

40. Ibid. 10, 199.

41. Iust., *Apol.* II.10.3.

42. Ibid. II.13.3., ANF 1, 193.

43. See: Clem. Al., *Str.* VII.VIII. 59.5.

We should take a look at what Saint Irenaeus, bishop of Lyons, had to say: "And faith is produced by the truth; for faith rests on things that truly are. For in things that are, as they are, we believe; and believing in things that are, as they ever are, we keep firm our confidence in them. Since then faith is the perpetuation of our salvation, we must needs bestow much pains on the maintenance thereof, in order that we may have a true comprehension of the things that are."[44] This is the true, dispassionate view of reality, the unfulfilled Stoic postulate of: *katalepsis ton onton*! This view, and there is universal agreement upon this, can only be reached through the teaching passed on by the apostles. Despite all their differences Justin agrees with Tertullian when it comes to this issue. There is only one real philosophy which leads to the knowledge of God and results in sanctity. The philosophers do not know this philosophy: "What philosophy is, however, and the reason why it has been sent down to men, have escaped the observation of most; for there would be neither Platonists, nor Stoics, nor Peripatetics, nor Theoretics, nor Pythagoreans, this knowledge being one."[45] Thereby the uniqueness of Christianity as the way of perfection is preserved. "And yet it is the truth," says Tertullian, "which is so troublesome to the world, that these philosophers affect, but which Christians possess."[46] "But straightway a flame was kindled in my soul," writes Justin about his conversion, "and a love of the prophets, and of those men who are friends of Christ, possessed me; and whilst revolving his words in my mind, I found this philosophy alone to be safe and profitable."[47]

44. Iren., *Demonstr.* 3 in Lay, *Readings in Historical Theology*, 69.

45. Iust., *Dial.* 2.1. ANF 1, 195.

46. Tert., *Nat.* I.4., ANF 3, 112.

47. Iust., *Dial.* 8.1. ANF 1, 198.

4

Selection and Adaptation

There is then in philosophy, though stolen as the fire by Prometheus, a slender spark, capable of being fanned into flame, a trace of wisdom and an impulse from God.[1]

In Christianity, opinion, while a raw material, is called philosophy of scholasticism; when a rejected refuse, it is called heresy.[2]

THE QUESTION OF HOW to use the philosophical, scientific, and literary tradition of the ancient world is not an exclusively Christian problem. It is a question within ancient philosophy itself of choosing the necessary or useful instruments for attaining the main goal of happiness and perfection. The various models of philosophical *paideia* developed from judgments about the many branches of knowledge and the arts, more specifically, from judgments about their usefulness for spiritual development. The emblematic example is Plato's revulsion toward poetry, which he not only saw as useless, but also harmful to spiritual development.[3] Different visions of human nature, its highest good,

1. Clem. Al., *Str.* I.XVII.87.1, ANF 2, 320.

2. Newman, *On the Development of Christian Doctrine*, 132.

3. To illustrate this point I will cite an extended passage from Cicero. Its immediate topic is the model of selection in the Epicurean school: "He seems to you to lack education: the reason is that he thought all education worthless which did not foster our learning to live happily. Should he have spent his time reading poetry . . . in which there is nothing of real use to be found but only childish amusement? Should he, like Plato, have wasted his days studying music, geometry, arithmetic, and astronomy? . . . And even if they were true, they have no bearing on whether we live more pleasantly, that is, better. Should he really have pursued those arts, and neglected the greatest and most difficult, and thereby the most fruitful art of all, the art of life? It is not Epicurus who is uneducated, but those who think that topics fit for a child to have learned should be

and the happiness that flows from it (we should not forget the diagnoses of the greatest causes of human sufferings, fears, humiliations, and discord) stood behind the specific criteria of selection. The task of all philosophy, including Christian philosophy, is the therapy of souls who have been led astray by the demands of the passions and false pictures of happiness. By differing in their opinions about starting points, and their visions of philosophy's goals, the philosophical schools also differed in their choices of therapy, their sets of exercises for enabling the soul to realize its natural perfection. The doubts of the Christians when it comes to this selection process in no way differs from those of the Platonists, Peripatetics, Epicureans, or Stoics as they pertain to evaluating the usefulness of particular fields of philosophy or, more widely, the value of the cultural heritage of antiquity. The goal (*telos*) and perfection (*teleiosis*) constitute the vistas of Greek philosophy and are the most substantial criteria of selection. When the Christians rejected pagan philosophy as an alternative way of life, it could no longer be an object of interest in itself. The consequence of ignoring what I have outlined is not only the abandoning of the doctrinal frames of Christianity, but also the actual embrace of another way of life, that is, of a goal entirely different than the one proposed by Christianity. It seems to me this is how we should understand the utterance in the famous dream of a great enthusiast of Cicero, Saint Jerome, who heard the following bitter words pronounced from the throne of God: *Ciceronianus es, non Christianus* [Cicero, not a Christian].[4]

The functional character of philosophy decided its attractiveness. Independently of the differences in opinion about human nature, of the highest good and the highest goal, Christians could not overlook the actual *consensus sapientium* in essential questions such as, for example, battling with the passions, which the philosophers saw as the foundation of spiritual transformation. The ancient spiritual exercises offer an immensely rich repertoire of means potentially useful on the way to sanctity and salvation. It is a given that no range of adaptation negated the clear conviction that revelation is the sole means to salvation. The unanimous consensus is: salvation suffices! What then, ask the radicals, is the use of reading astronomy, logic, and practicing Stoic meditation techniques if revelation is the fullness of knowledge and does not need to be supplemented by anything? This is how the question of the value of antiquity's culture opens the doors to the Christian life. We will examine certain aspects of the mechanisms that eventually resulted in some ancient Christians being incapable of imagining authentic sanctity without the ancient pagan philosophical exercises. In addition, in some instances the

---

studied until old age." Cic., *Fin.* I.27.71–72, 25.

4. See: Hier., *Epist.* XXII.30.

life of a simple Christian seemed decidedly inferior to them in comparison with the both the perfection of a Christian hermit practicing Stoic-inspired *ascesis* and the perfection of a monk-intellectual who was using dialectics.

In the fourth century the principle of selection found its intellectual outlet in the writings of Saints Augustine and Jerome.[5] Yet, even before Augustine formulated his mature doctrine of adaptation and selection in his dialogue *On Order*[6] and in his treatise *On Christian Teaching*, Christians already applied it in practice. This is obvious. Just to take one of many such exemplary thinkers: in the *Apology* Aristides unequivocally established the criteria for knowledge of what is necessary for salvation. He argued that it was useful for a believer to know, for example, about the absurdities of barbarian and pagan theologies.[7] Continual adaptation and selection were daily necessities for Christians who all lived in a pagan environment. All of the following factors required intelligible and unequivocal ways of judging their value: the luster of ancient culture, contacts with pagans, the baggage of habits carried over by converts, the Bible's lack of clarity, the explosion of philosophical Gnosticism, intellectual curiosity, and the problem of defining a Christian upbringing.

Two Variants of the Exercises

Revelation ultimately resolves the issue of the final goal of human life, but it does not discuss many specific questions pertaining to human nature. Chadwick summarizes it thus, "The New Testament writers do not philosophize and we may think this a fact of providential importance since in consequence the gospel is not inextricably associated with a first-century metaphysical structure. Its relationship to philosophy has therefore detachment which is to the clear advantage of both sides."[8] Christianity might owe its variety of legitimate paths, or as Clement of Alexandria puts it, streams that feed the current of a river, to this very detachment from any particular philosophy.[9] This variety would have been unthinkable had Constantine chosen to impose the Stoic, Epicurean, or Platonic ways of life, and their attendant restrictions,

5. Domański, "Patrystyczne postawy wobec dziedzictwa antycznego"[Patristic Stands toward the Heritage of Antiquity], 16–18.

6. This small treatise can be seen as a program for educating a Christian sage. In it Augustine recommends the study of music, geometry, astronomy, and mathematics, all helpful in the discovery and contemplation of the divine order of the world.

7. See: Arist., *Apol.* 1–3; 8.

8. Chadwick, *Early Christian Thought and the Classical Tradition*, 4–5.

9. See: Clem. Al., *Str.* I.V.29.3. The Bible, Clement argues, speaks of "several ways of salvation" in Clem., *Str.* I.V.29.3, ANF 2, 304.

upon his empire after the Battle of Milvian Bridge. And so it is not just a matter of what would have been the official philosophy of the empire, but also what elements of the pagan heritage would have been decisively excluded. It is possible that dialectic (Cynics) would have been excluded, or poetry (Plato), while everyone, without exception, including the butcher and tailor, would have been required to learn astronomy, geometry, or music. The varieties of Christianity, incomprehensible to the Greek spirit, point toward a certain non-rigorous optimism, which gives expression to the belief that the world is essentially good and so the greatest works of humanity could not have come into being without God's will and God's inspiration.

Early Christians put different emphases upon the proportions in which praxis and theory should coexist in human nature and its perfection by taking advantage of the realm of freedom given to them. The ancient philosophers were generally the ultimate guides in making these choices, even though their presence was discrete and nearly imperceptible. We should take a look at two substantial currents of Christian inquiries. The first, influenced by a Platonism filtered through Stoicism, considered the highest function of human nature to be the divinization of humanity, which realized itself in the act of intellectual contemplation. The second, inspired by the Roman Stoics, saw the pinnacle of human life, and its form of divinization, in the long path toward God in a disciplined and reasonable life wholly devoted to the guidance of virtue. Each one of these schools obviously chose different paths of selecting useful exercises for realizing their respective ideals. Each one claimed priority for itself, not without suspiciously eyeing its competitor. Yet, both options clearly fit within the confines of the church.

Justin Martyr: The Greek Variety

Justin Martyr, who earned two titles for himself, those of Philosopher and Martyr, was the patron of the first option. It was his conviction that the good of philosophy consisted in its function as a guide toward God: "philosophy is, in fact, the greatest possession, and most honourable before God, to whom it leads us and alone commends us; and these are truly holy men who have bestowed attention on philosophy."[10] This was a declaration that could have been made by the students of any pagan philosophical school toward the middle of the second century. We know that in truth, according to Justin, Christianity is the only certain and useful philosophy.[11] Now it will be our task to establish

---

10. Iust., *Dial.* 2.1, ANF 1, 195.

11. Ibid. 8.1.

just what constituted the perfection/holiness of the people that were led toward God by Christian philosophy.

Justin joined the church after a period when he was strongly engaged in Platonism.[12] Before this period, as he admits, he encountered the Stoics, Peripatetics, and Pythagoreans. The spiritual autobiography he nestled within the *Dialogue with Trypho* demonstrates how well Christianity realized the hopes and wants awakened by philosophy.[13] Justin confesses he converted because he witnessed the unyielding courage of Christians facing martyrdom, meaning, he was influenced by a proof of the authenticity of Christian teaching that could easily be expressed by a philosophical vocabulary used at the time by both the Stoics and the Platonists.[14] "For I myself, too, when I was delighting in the doctrines of Plato, and heard the Christians slandered, and saw them fearless of death, and of all other-things which are counted fearful, perceived that it was impossible that they could be living in wickedness and pleasure."[15] The attitude he noticed in the simple disciples of Christ corresponded to one of the most important characteristics of the sage in nearly all the philosophical schools of antiquity. We must not forget how this corresponds to an extremely elite philosophical ideal, thought to be in principle unattainable for ordinary adepts of philosophy, and only then will we understand Justin's reaction to the witness of the most ordinary members of the Christian community.

Therefore, Justin's attitudes toward philosophy are clearly influenced by the sense of the spiritual continuity with his own path, by the family resemblance between philosophical questions and the language of faith, that is, a language in which the author of the *Apology* received a satisfactory answer and a conviction about the substantial philosophical reasons behind his inner transformation. Justin would surely agree with Saint Paul who in his speech assured the Athenian philosophers they worship what they do not know·and that it is the same thing the Christians are preaching to them (Acts 17:23). Justin said, "For I myself, when I discovered the wicked disguise which the evil spirits had thrown around the divine doctrines of the Christians, to turn aside others from joining them, laughed both at those who framed these falsehoods, and at the disguise itself and at popular opinion and I confess that I both boast and with all my strength strive to be found a Christian; not because the teachings of Plato are different from those of Christ, but because they are not

---

12. For the consequences of this move see: Edwards, "On the Platonic Schooling of Justin Martyr," 17–34.

13. Iust., *Dial.* 2.1–8.2. See also: Chadwick, *History and Thought of the Early Church*, 161, 277.

14. See: Osborn, *Justin Martyr*, 81–82 and Nock, *Conversion*, 107–8, 254–55.

15. Iust., *Apol.* II.12.1–3, ANF 1, 192.

in all respects similar, as neither are those of the others, Stoics, and poets, and historians."[16] It is impossible to doubt that the philosophical experiences not only predated but also conditioned his conversion. Therefore, even if Justin sins a bit through his lack of clarity when it comes distinguishing between the popular philosophy of his time and Christianity, then he himself is a living proof that Greek philosophy can be conceived as both *praeparatio evangelica* [preparation for the gospel], and as a spiritual aid for the deepening of the Christian faith.[17] Whenever Greek philosophy is put on trial Justin Martyr's personal history is the best witness for the defense of philosophy for one more reason: Justin himself died as a martyr and thereby proved the completeness of his conversion both in the categories of Greek philosophy and the gospel.

It is not a coincidence that Justin penned his tract on the adaptability of the popular Platonism of his time in the form of a philosophical dialogue.[18] The meeting with the elderly man described in the *Dialogue*, which aims to point out the main similarities and differences, is an important lesson in the spiritual unity of the world in which the ancient church matured. The process of adoption here is something like the critical selection of the dowry that a former student of Plato brings to the church through his conversion. And so the elderly man does not find too many opportunities to disagree with Justin. During the philosopher's long lecture his interlocutor only protests twice: the first time when not enough due is given to grace in the process of coming to know God,[19] and the second time in a reaction against the doctrine of the preexistence and migration of souls, which is attacked more methodically.[20] Both of these theses were rejected on the basis of philosophical arguments (i.e., the moral absurdity of the teaching of reincarnation, or the inadequacy of human knowledge), and not on the basis of scripture.

The philosophical dowry of Justin consists of an immense number of indisputable theological theses. In theology this heritage consists in the agreement to call God the cause of all things (3.5), the belief in his transcendence

16. Ibid. II.12.1–3, ANF 1, 192–93.

17. As Clement said, "But if the Hellenic philosophy comprehends not the whole extent of the truth, and besides is destitute of strength to perform the commandments of the Lord, yet it prepares the way for the truly royal teaching; training in some way or other, and moulding the character, and fitting him who believes in Providence for the reception of the truth." Clem. Al., *Str.* I.XVI.80.6, ANF 2, 318.

18. "There is too much dramatic and literary finesse for the conversation to be merely the result of a good memory, one thing which we know that Justin did not possess," says Osborn, *Justin Martyr*, 7.

19. Iust., *Dial.* 4.1–4.

20. Ibid. 4.5—5.2.

(he remains beyond being, is unknowable through the senses, and is ineffable), and the belief in his eternity and immutability. It is indubitable that God is both beauty and the good (4.1). The role of reason, which rules over everything, is especially unchallenged, in addition, neither is the goal of humanity to strive toward morally perfected knowledge about the essence of things, meaning, toward wisdom understood as a knowledge of the truth that leads to true happiness (3.4).[21]

The epistemological presuppositions are especially interesting from our own perspective.[22] Both interlocutors agree knowledge is a name common to many things. Knowledge of divine and human things differs and outranks knowledge such as the knowledge of music, arithmetic, or astronomy. If we gain this ordinary knowledge through study and certain forms of intellectual exercise, then we can attain God in one of two ways, of which only the first has the luster of true philosophical knowledge. That is, we can come to know God either intuitively, directly, through an act of intellectual seeing (by relying upon the eye of the soul, as Justin puts it, following Plato), or also *ex auditu*, meaning, through the mediation of those who have this direct knowledge (3.6—4.1).

The discussion concludes with a demonstration of how inconsequential and weak the Platonic teaching about the soul really is, since it only confirms that the knowledge philosophers have of things human and divine should not be trusted. Justin is convinced that philosophy does not rest upon certain knowledge *ex visione*, nor even upon reliable secondhand knowledge, and so he asks the elderly gentleman for help.[23] What to do? Where to start? Whom to lean on when even the philosophers cannot be trusted? The elderly man leans upon the witness of prophets, who have seen the truth and have revealed it to others. His answer combines unmediated witness with the concept of grace. The prophets only spoke, "those things alone which they saw and which they

---

21. "[T]he majority of men will not, saving such as shall live justly, purified by righteousness, and by every other virtue." Actually, even though Justin's interlocutor probably had the problem of grace in mind, as he exhibits doubts about the conclusion that reason and virtue are a sufficient conditions for knowing God (ibid. 4.2–4), there is no doubt that he considers them necessary conditions: "'Is there then,' says he, 'such and so great power in our mind? Or can a man not perceive by sense sooner? Will the mind of man see God at any time, if it is uninstructed by the Holy Spirit?'" Ibid. 4.1, ANF 1, 196.

22. See: Osborn, *Justin Martyr*, 66–76.

23. "'How then,' he said, 'should the philosophers judge correctly about God, or speak any truth, when they have no knowledge of Him, having neither seen Him at any time, nor heard Him?'" Iust., *Dial.* 3.7, ANF 1, 196.

heard, being filled with the Holy Spirit."[24] Their writings constitute a reliable source of knowledge about all things that might preoccupy a philosopher.[25]

As we can see the most important element in Justin's stance is his meta-philosophical approach. The interlocutors both agree that the most substantial goal of human life is the complete metamorphosis of being and knowledge, which is crowned by a direct "seeing" of God. The adaptation completes itself with an overcoming of philosophy, in effect, with a decision to fight the enemy with their weapons and on their soil. The pagan masters of Justin are discredited with the help of a philosophical ideal that they cannot attain. The acknowledgment of this ideal as the form of Christian perfection is the consequence of the victory. In this way the Platonic path from opinions to *epistēmē* comes to serve the description of a Christian path to salvation. It is impossible to overestimate the importance of this decision.

As we have pointed out earlier, in the many philosophical schools Justin encountered, the starting point for spiritual work (philosophizing) was a faith in the authority of the writings and sayings of a given school's founder. The ancients, especially after the lesson the skeptics taught them, had serious reservations about any Cartesian methods of spiritual transformation, that is, ones marked by obviousness and certainty at every step.[26] This clearly does not mean that successive stages of spiritual transformation are totally incomprehensible or irrational to an adept. However, only a full conversion will give them a direct, and seemingly unmediated, knowledge that will confirm the chosen path. For all the philosophical schools the fullness of knowledge, truth, and certainty was attainable only at the end of the spiritual exercises, independently of how the various schools conceived the obviousness and inter-subjective accountability of successive steps of epistemological and moral development. It seems to me this pattern holds the answer to the question

24. Ibid. 7.1–2, 198.

25. When Justin asks the elderly man to reveal the source of his teaching, the elderly man does not rely upon his own intellectual witness, he instead opts for the authority of the prophets and their scriptures. We can understand this as meaning the scriptures constitute the path toward perfection that realizes itself in contemplation of God, or we can also understand it as meaning that intellectual seeing was only given to the prophets while the perfection of a Christian expresses itself in the observation of the teachings they have left behind in the scriptures. Most likely Justin combines both these possibilities by treating the scriptures as a vehicle that can bring the chosen to perfection crowned by the contemplation of God.

26. Nock, *Conversion*, 181 stressed the role trust in masters and loyalty toward a school's tradition played in ancient philosophy: "The philosopher commonly said not 'Follow my arguments one by one: check and control them to the best of your ability: truth should be dearer than Plato to you,' but 'Look at this picture which I paint \, and can you resist its attractions?'"

of how Justin conceived the difference between the starting and end points of the Christian path, between knowledge and faith, between the Bible as a path for contemplating God and the Bible as the rule of a just life—it is a very important question from the perspective of the logic of adopting the ancient philosophical exercises.

One can say knowledge differs from faith not through its content, but through a person. The ancients used a subjective, or existential, concept of knowledge, which is an obvious consequence of philosophy understood as both a moral and epistemological transformation. If epistemology utilizes the analogy between intellectual knowledge and seeing, then, as a consequence, knowledge is not only, or even not above all, a system of objectified truths (that can be passed on or heard), instead it is the state of a mind seeing the truth. This is how a sage differs from an ignoramus: by what he *is*, rather than by what he knows. When the sage possesses the truth he becomes its personification and his life is both an effect of this process and proves the authenticity of the pointers toward perfection, "For they did not use demonstration in their treatises, seeing that they were witnesses to the truth above all demonstration, and worthy of belief . . . ."[27] The content of the scriptures is therefore objectively real and it is the very same content for both the person who believes and for the one who knows God through intellectual seeing. The writings of the prophets "are still extant, and he who has read them is very much helped in his knowledge of the beginning and end of things, and of those matters which the philosopher ought to know."[28] The content of the scriptures for those who are not sages, can only be the object of faith, because it is deprived of the certainty gained through direct knowledge. This obviously does not mean such faith is irrational. It can be accepted because of the witness of the saints, the credibility of the prophets, and cosmological arguments.[29] Faith is not so much unintelligible, but instead none of the arguments in its favor have the same intellectual obviousness, which is only available through direct knowledge of God. Faith can be treated as a lower ranking knowledge, which is not yet a lasting state of seeing the object of knowledge. Faith is the knowledge of a man who finds himself at the starting blocks of spiritual change, a man upon the first stage of succeeding approximations whose objective value can only be properly evaluated through the perspective of a completed journey toward the full truth.

Even before his conversion Justin says,

27. Iust., *Dial.* 7.2, ANF 1, 198.

28. Ibid. 7.2, ANF 1, 198.

29. See: Daniélou, *Gospel Message and Hellenistic Culture*, 211–20; Chadwick, *History and Thought of the Early Church*, 288–89; Skarsaune, *The Proof from Prophecy*.

But without philosophy and right reason, prudence would not be present to any man. Wherefore it is necessary for every man to philosophize, and to esteem this the greatest and most honourable work; but other things only of second-rate or third-rate importance, though, indeed, if they be made to depend on philosophy, they are of moderate value, and worthy of acceptance; but deprived of it, and not accompanying it, they are vulgar and coarse to those who pursue them.[30]

It appears this opinion did not lose any of its force after his conversion. Despite such declarations Justin himself remained somewhat restrained about including the ancient philosophical exercises in the armory of Christian contemplation. We can conclude from his pre-Christian experiences that he unwillingly reached for the conclusion that extensive intellectual exercises are a necessary precondition for the contemplation of God. In the *Dialogue* he recalls how a Pythagorean he studied under recommended Justin take up the study of music, astronomy, and geometry. This Pythagorean asked rhetorically, "Do you expect to perceive any of those things which conduce to a happy life, if you have not been first informed on those points which wean the soul from sensible objects, and render it fitted for objects which appertain to the mind, so that it can contemplate that which is honourable in its essence and that which is good in its essence?"[31] The impatient Justin considered all this an unnecessary delay. But already for Clement of Alexandria Justin's ambition to "become acquainted with the Christ of God, and, after being initiated, live a happy life," would be very difficult to realize without this preparatory phase.[32]

Perfection according to Clement

The assertion that Platonic philosophy provides the proper background for the Pauline division between spiritual infants (*nēpioi*) and those who stand higher in Christian development creates a climate in which the adaptation of philosophical spiritual exercises seems like something entirely natural.[33] However, the use of philosophy in the work of salvation can introduce some dangerous divisions within the church. The first difficulty surfaces from the clash between the elite nature of philosophical culture and the universality of the Christian promise of salvation directed at everyone independently of

---

30. Iust., *Dial.* 3.3, ANF 1, 196.
31. Ibid. 2.4, ANF 1, 195.
32. Ibid. 8.2, ANF 1, 198.
33. See: 1 Cor 3:2 and Heb 5:12—6:1; Clem. Al., *Str.* I.XXVII.179.2.

their education or intellectual talents. Second, it creates dangerous and wholly unacceptable analogies with gnostic divisions between the mere psychics, who were unworthy of salvation, and the pneumatics who were not subject to sin because they were saved already in this life by knowledge unavailable to the profane.

Clement understood how intellectual elitism posed a mortal threat to the gospel, both in its milder professorial-snobbish version and in its more acute form of the gnostic promise of self-salvation for those who possess esoteric knowledge. But Clement, a scholar of the Alexandrian catechetical school, noted one more danger.[34] It comes from the arrogant conviction that the grace of faith frees one from the difficulty of spiritual work. Clement's adaptation of philosophy combines these two observations. They are not debatable, because faith is sufficient for salvation and human weakness also means nothing is ever given forever—one must continually work in order to cultivate and develop a treasure that can be easily lost.[35]

But is philosophy still really needed? Or has revelation suspended it? What use is there for partial truth when the whole truth is given by Christ?[36] Even if we acknowledge the great contributions of philosophy, admitting it was a type of preparatory knowledge (*propaideia*),[37] meaning that philosophy was a way for God to prepare the Greeks to accept the gospel, can we reasonably argue that a grown person should return to the kindergarten of faith? This is a very difficult question, especially since we would also have to accept, as Clement sees it, all the errors and contradictions the pride of philosophers injected into a teaching the Greeks did not invent themselves, because they either received this teaching through a special revelation passed on to the chosen or they stole it from the prophets.[38] And yet is it possible to be a Christian without philosophy? Can we really say all of it is of no value?

On the Utility of Pagan Philosophy

Clement says with some bite, "Some, who think themselves naturally gifted, do not wish to touch either philosophy or logic; nay more, they do not wish to

34. Michalski, *Antologia Literatury Patrystycznej* [Anthology of Patristic Literature], Vol. 1, 332, mentions the similarity of this first Christian theological academy to ancient philosophical schools. Anyone can confirm this by reading Gregory Thaumaturgus's *In Praise of Origen* (ANF 6). See: Hadot, *Philosophy as a Way of Life*, 163–64.

35. See: Henry Chadwick, *Early Christian Thought and the Classical Tradition*, 47–49.

36. Clem. Al., *Str.* VI.X.83.1.

37. Ibid. VI.VII.62.1.

38. See: ibid. I.XVIII.94.1–4.

learn natural science. They demand bare faith alone, as if they wished, without bestowing any care on the vine, straightway to gather clusters from the first."[39] The truth, that is, the teaching of the Savior is indubitably "complete in itself without defect."[40] This is not debatable. Faith is sufficient for salvation. The question is whether we can last in it without any philosophical support. The inaccessibility of the truth is no longer a problem after the revelation of God. The problem now is ordering our lives, desires, habits, and limitations so that the act of conversion will last, that is, whether it will become a stable disposition of our body and spirit. This opens up a space for philosophical skills and exercises. Philosophy, the mistress of moral and intellectual training, becomes useful when it protects, strengthens, and develops the graces of faith. Therefore, Clement proposes a program of Christian eclecticism so the baby does not get thrown out with the bathwater. Should we not use every form of teaching to unearth elements that are useful for the faith?[41] Perhaps philosophy should be treated instrumentally, plundered for whatever might be helpful along the way toward salvation? Clement says, "[By] philosophy—I do not mean the Stoic, or the Platonic, or the Epicurean, or the Aristotelian, but whatever has been well said by each of those sects, which teach righteousness along with a science pervaded by piety,—this eclectic whole I call philosophy."[42] If we act in the following way, "For the teaching which is agreeable to Christ deifies the Creator, and traces providence in particular events, and knows the nature of the elements to be capable of change and production, and teaches that we ought to aim at rising up to the power which assimilates to God [as in Plato's *Theaetetus* 176b], and to prefer the dispensation as holding the first rank and superior to all training," then the danger of false selections seems to disappear.[43]

39. Ibid. I.IX.43.1, ANF 2, 309.

40. Ibid. I.XX.100.1, ANF 2, 323.

41. Ibid. VI.X.80.1.

42. Ibid. I.VII.37.6, ANF 2, 308. See also: Daniélou, *Gospel Message and Hellenistic Culture*, 309. The justification for this move comes from how such a sifting allows the believer to see the whole lost by the adulterations of Greek philosophers. "Since, therefore, truth is one (for falsehood has ten thousand by-paths); just as the Bacchantes tore asunder the limbs of Pentheus, so the sects both of barbarian and Hellenic philosophy have done with truth, and each vaunts as the whole truth the portion which has fallen to its lot. But all, in my opinion, are illuminated by the dawn of Light. Let all, therefore, both Greeks and barbarians, who have aspired after the truth,—both those who possess not a little, and those who have any portion,—produce whatever they have of the word of truth." Clem. Al., *Str.* I.XIII.57.6, ANF 2, 313.

43. Ibid. I.XI.52.3–4, 312.

In his discussions with the Christian opponents of using philosophy Clement does not abstract from the living realities of a church submerged in an unfavorably disposed pagan world. The main value of a well-grounded education is the help it can give in the defense of the faith. Should we not bring any implements to cultivate the vineyard? Do we not discount the athlete who comes unprepared?[44] Clement snarls, seeing how the positions of some Christians gave opponents of the church a monopoly on using philosophy. The faith cannot be defended by plugging up one's ears at the sound of a Siren song.[45] After all, what good is a faith its opponents can turn to dust?[46] Philosophy becomes useful even when we can explain its uselessness as Clement points out (borrowing from Aristotle's *Protrepticus*). However, we need to deeply engage philosophy before we can make such an argument. Only then will we be able to take advantage of what in it is "a divine gift to the Greeks," and learn to avoid all the dangerous traps.[47]

The realities of evangelization also come into play here. Even if the study of philosophy is not necessary to reach the ultimate goal, then it can help the ascent toward the goal by criticizing pagan culture. The work of teaching is one simple example, "And otherwise erudition commends him, who sets forth the most essential doctrines so as to produce persuasion in his hearers, engendering admiration in those who are taught, and leads them to the truth."[48]

Philosophy not only defends one from external enemies, but from internal ones as well. Only a thorough education can be a benchmark for distinguishing sophistry from philosophy, rhetoric from dialectic, and authentic Christianity from heresy. And how is it possible to deal with troubling biblical passages without the aid of philosophy?[49] Of course it is true that the apostles and prophets did not know philosophy, but as pupils of the Spirit they were able to grasp the meaning of the faith directly. Unfortunately, this would be much more difficult for Clement's contemporaries if they do not have the

---

44. Ibid. I.IX.43.4.

45. Ibid. VI.XI.89.1.

46. Ibid. VI.X.80.1.

47. Ibid. I.II.20.2, 303. Like Clement, Justin Martyr also ponders why philosophy was sent down to men in *Dial.* 2.1, "What philosophy is, however, and the reason why it has been sent down to men, have escaped the observation of most; for there would be neither Platonists, nor Stoics, nor Peripatetics, nor Theoretics, nor Pythagoreans, this knowledge being one." Iust., *Dial.* 2.1, ANF 1, 195.

48. Clem. Al., *Str.* I.II.19.4, ANF 2, 30.

49. Ibid. I.IX.44.1–4.

proper philosophical training. After all, not everyone is able to consciously receive the Lord's teaching without the help of expert explanations.[50]

Faith, *Gnōsis*, Love

These are the starting points for outlining a portrait of Clement's ideal of a Christian gnostic: a follower of Jesus who through intellectual exercises, with the help of God, can achieve the fullness of perfection available to man. The ability to defend the faith and avoid evil are only the beginning. The gnostic is not satisfied with doing the good out of fear or in the hope of a reward. The gnostic does the good through love with regard only for the moral good.[51] Rewards are not the goal, but *gnōsis* in itself.[52] When underscoring disinterestedness Clement does not shrink from formulating a paradox that sounds shocking coming from a Christian. If we hypothetically assume that knowledge of God, meaning *gnōsis*, and the salvation of the soul do not constitute an indivisible whole then the gnostic would choose the truth instead of salvation.[53] This kind of knowledge is one of the central elements of transforming one's being. The gnostic strives to make awareness of God a constant state, an eternal contemplation of God, something belonging to the very core of his being.[54] Similarly, the doing of the good should become a lasting disposition (*hexis*) of his nature.[55] "As is right, then, knowledge itself loves and teaches the ignorant, and instructs the whole creation to honour God Almighty. And if such an one teaches to love God, he will not hold virtue as a thing to be lost in any case, either awake or in a dream, or in any vision; since the habit never goes out of itself by falling from being a habit."[56] Knowledge (*gnōsis*) is the process of man perfecting himself through knowledge of divine things, a process that manifests itself in his whole disposition, thinking, and way of life. A person, who comes to the end of this process, reaches a point of perfect

50. Clement says, "And if the prophets and apostles knew not the arts by which the exercises of philosophy are exhibited, yet the mind of the prophetic and instructive spirit, uttered secretly, because all have not an intelligent ear, demands skillful modes of teaching in order to clear exposition." Ibid. I.IX.45.1, ANF 2, 310.

51. Ibid. IV.XXII.135.1–4.

52. The meaning of the term *gnōsis* in Clement is discussed by Lilla, *Clement of Alexandria*, 142–89.

53. Clem. Al., *Str.* IV.XXII.136.1–5.

54. Ibid. IV.XXII.136.4.

55. Ibid. IV.XXII.138.3–4.

56. Ibid. IV.XXII.139.203, ANF 2, 435.

inner harmony, which is a harmony with the Word of God.[57] It is the highest degree of assimilating oneself to God available to man.[58] The Platonic ideal of divinization gains concrete and real qualities through its encounter with Christianity. For Clement, the ideal of the gnostic, which fully actualizes the ancient ideal of the sage, is Christ.[59]

The relationship of such an understanding of *gnōsis* to simple faith is such that through knowledge (*gnōsis*) the believer becomes a fully actualized person.[60] Faith is a simple act of knowledge, thanks to which, independently of all research, we come to know and acknowledge God, loving him as a present reality.[61] Faith is an indispensable condition for both salvation and knowledge: "In the first place, it is a choice between death and life, between sin and salvation. . . . In the second place the decision of faith is a choice between perpetual ignorance and the possibility of knowledge."[62] Conversion constitutes the subjective condition for knowledge, it equips the believer with new ears and eyes with which he can come to know God. Through accepting the Greek epistemological principle that the like can only be known by the like, Clement identifies faith as the precondition for the possibility of any knowledge, because faith is the first step of a process that likens man to God.[63] "Thus, the truth is given within faith, and this truth is Christ. . . . But there is the task of understanding the truth which is already known."[64] This is why faith ought to be recognized as the starting point, as it is a type of an elementary coming to know God, which, with the help of grace, can be taken to a higher level, to *gnōsis* understood as a divinizing contemplation of God. What is interesting is that, for Clement, faith is also a starting point for knowledge as a systematic collection of judgments linked through the principles of logic. We could say that the first conversion is a conversion from paganism to faith, while the second conversion is from faith to knowledge.[65] It is interesting that in the order of logic (it is inseparable from spirituality in the life of a gnostic) faith

57. Ibid. VII.X.55.1.

58. See: Butterworth, "The Deification of Man in Clement of Alexandria," 157–69.

59. Clem. Al., *Str.* I.V.21.1.

60. Ibid. VII.X.55.2.

61. Ibid. VII.X.55.2.

62. Osborn, *The Philosophy of Clement of Alexandria*, 127–28.

63. Ibid., 128–31. Osborn considers this to be an original interpretation of the widely accepted principle that presupposed virtue as the necessary precondition for intellectual knowledge. Osborn points out analogies with *Phaedo* 64c-65a; *Rep.* 402; 500; 518; 533; *Theaet.* 176c.

64. Daniélou, *Gospel Message and Hellenistic Culture*, 312.

65. Clem. Al., *Str.* VII.X.57.4.

is an axiom that cannot be reduced to more fundamental presuppositions and it lies at the foundations of systematic knowledge about the divine.[66] Granted, the truth of this axiom is only confirmed through the effects of accepting the initial axiomatic certainty. As Eric Osborn puts it, "The demonstration follows after faith, not faith after the demonstration."[67] The fullness of knowledge and the certainty that accompanies it comes only at the end of the road. We should point out that faith as an initial orientation also distinguishes *gnōsis* from the knowledge one can acquire in school. *Gnōsis* does contain some elements of academic knowledge, but it is obviously not identical with it. Whoever does not accept the gift of faith, even if extraordinarily learned, thereby blocks the door to perfection. Love is the goal of this path and that also cannot be taught in a classroom. Therefore, both the beginning and the end of spiritual development, being a gift of God, pass through the fingers of teaching methods. Christ is the beginning and the end, "And the extreme points, the beginning and the end—I mean faith and love—are not taught."[68]

Spiritual Exercises

Where there is God we are able to elevate ourselves through faith, *gnōsis*, and love. *Gnōsis*, always with the aid of grace, is only transmitted to a select few students who are ready for it. It requires special provisions and spiritual exercises, "on account of the necessity for very great preparation and previous training in order both to hear what is said, and for the composure of life, and for advancing intelligently to a point beyond the righteousness of the law."[69] All of this hinges upon humanity being created not as perfect, but as

---

66. Lilla, *Clement of Alexandria*, 119. For a discussion of the concept *pistis* (faith) look in the same volume 118–42 and Daniélou, *Gospel Message and Hellenistic Culture*, 310–20; Osborn, *The Emergence of Christian Thought*, 262–65. I follow Osborn, who distinguishes the moral-spiritual and logical meaning of *pistis* in Clement. He says the following about the latter, "Faith is the logical foundation of all knowledge. There can be no knowledge which is not based on faith. The first principles of knowledge cannot themselves be rationally demonstrated. Until they are somehow accepted there can be no knowledge. The acceptance of them is called faith. . . . One point to be noted is that Clement does not claim that the basic elements of Christian truth can be proved by the light of natural reason. He claims it is logically necessary that they cannot be proved (or disproved) by the light of natural reason. Knowledge must depend on something other than knowledge." See: Osborn, *The Philosophy of Clement of Alexandria*, 131 (For Osborn's whole argument see: ibid., 127–45).

67. Osborn, *The Philosophy of Clement of Alexandria*, 141.

68. Clem. Al., *Str.* VII.X.55.6, ANF 2, 538.

69. Ibid. VII.X.56.1–2, ANF 2, 539.

possessing the potential for virtue and knowledge.[70] Even though moral and intellectual developments of a gnostic must be equal, they are facilitated by totally different sets of exercises.

"All, then, as I said, are naturally constituted for the acquisition of virtue. But one man applies less, one more, to learning and training."[71] The Greeks, and Clement follows them, understand virtue (both intellectual and moral) as a certain skill or ability (*dynamis*). Ancient philosophy remains in the shadow of an immense discovery, which unveiled the role that habit plays in our spiritual life, that is, the stable predisposition, which, as Democritus said, is capable of becoming a second nature to man. The whole understanding of virtues and vices is essentially a conceptualization of the habits that we gain through frequent repetitions. Is it any wonder that the philosophy which leads to perfection is full of martial and athletic metaphors, and philosophy itself can be understood as a set of exercises (Greek: *askēsis*) that make the spirit more capable? We should remember that these exercises are mutually reinforcing. The development of moral virtues is a condition for deepening spiritual knowledge and vice-versa. The ideal is a state of totally sovereignty of mind, that is, the highest degree of freedom available to humanity from the limitations imposed by the body, "But we must, by acquiring superiority in the rational part, show ourselves masters of the inferior creation in us."[72]

Clement uses two Platonic definitions of philosophy to describe this ideal. The first comes from the *Phaedo*, and describes the goal negatively, meaning, it describes what a person must liberate himself from in order to achieve perfection: "suppose [the soul] is separated in purity, while trailing nothing of the body with it, since it had no avoidable commerce with it during life, but shunned it; suppose too that it has been gathered together alone into itself, since it always cultivated this—nothing else but the right practice of philosophy, in fact, the cultivation of dying without complaint—would not that be the cultivation of death?"[73] The positive definition borrows from the *Theaetetus* the ideal of likening oneself to God, a God who attracts the initiate with the hope of putting behind the world of change, uncertainty, constant

---

70. Eric Osborn, in *The Philosophy of Clement of Alexandria*, 146–54, as he does in the case of *pistis*, also divides gnostic knowledge into spiritual-moral and logical. The effects of the first are the development of the spiritual life and an increase in virtue; they are crowned by moral perfection and contemplation of God (Clem. Al., *Str.* VI.I.2.4). The second, which emerges from the axioms of faith, when ordered by logical discipline, leads to a systematized knowledge of God (ibid. VI.I.3.2).

71. Clem. Al., *Str.* VI.XII.96.3, ANF 2, 502.

72. Ibid. II.XX.114.1, ANF 2, 372.

73. Pl., *Phaedo* 80e–81a; see also: ibid. 67d–e.

becoming, and perishing for the divine impassibility and self-sufficiency of a sage who is like God.[74]

The Battle with the Passions

When it comes to the passions Clement is faithful to Saint Paul, but also to Plato and the Stoics. He sees the path to knowing as reducing the range of what escapes the control of reason. This is why the initial exercises in the gnostic way of life are, above all, exercises that aim to lastingly overcome the passions. These exercises, much like in the whole Greek tradition, depend upon limiting pleasures associated with bed and table, upon renouncing luxuries, upon fasts and vigils, which were supposed to train the soul in control, endurance, and detachment, thereby freeing her from being embarrassingly mastered by bodily needs.[75] The asceticism of Clement grows out of the Stoic tradition. Complete detachment from affect is this tradition's goal, and so Clement emphasizes, "And the complete eradication of desire reaps as its fruit impassibility."[76] The Alexandrian not only denies the lower desires any right to exist in the soul, but also sadness, happiness, and anger.[77] It is easy to spot how many great ancient witnesses—from Euripides to Antisthenes and from Xenophanes to Plato—support the Christian theologian in his striving toward a salvation by way of many helpful maxims, upbuilding examples, weighty arguments and exercises.[78]

As Pierre Hadot puts it, spiritual exercises almost always required "attention to one's self . . . [which was the] very definition of the monastic attitude."[79] Constant spiritual vigilance is the responsibility of someone who practices *ascēsis*; it is reminiscent of the Stoic practice of paying attention to the soul (*prosochē*).[80] Clement follows Saint Paul (1 Thess 5:6–8) in admonishing the gnostic to not sleep as the others do.[81] The uninterrupted vigilance of reason and perseverance in fighting the passions eventually transform themselves

---

74. See: Pl., *Tht.* 176b; Pl., *R.* 613a–b.

75. See: the intermittent discussions of *ascēsis* in the chapter "Christianity as Revealed Philosophy" in Hadot, *What is Ancient Philosophy?*, 237–52.

76. Clem. Al., *Str.* VI.IX.74.2, ANF 2, 497.

77. Ibid. VI.IX.71.1–77.

78. See: ibid. II.XX.103–126.4.

79. Hadot, *What is Ancient Philosophy?*, 242.

80. Hadot, *Philosophy as a Way of Life*, 84–85.

81. Clem. Al., *Str.* IV.XXII.140.3.

into self-control as a constant disposition of the gnostic's soul.[82] "Wherefore the divine law," writes Clement, "appears to me necessarily to menace with fear (*eulabeia*), that, by caution and attention (*prosochē*), the philosopher may acquire and retain absence of anxiety (*amerimnia*), continuing without fall and without sin in all things."[83] "This passage implies," says Pierre Hadot, "the whole thought-world of ancient philosophy. The divine law is both the *logos* of the philosophers and the Christian *Logos*. It inspires circumspection in action, prudence, and attention to oneself—that is to say, the fundamental Stoic attitude. These in turn procure peace of mind, an inner disposition sought by all the schools."[84]

Exercises of Reason

The faculty of knowledge, which is tied to reason and its control over the passions, like the reason it depends upon, is not automatically given to humans. "And as knowledge (*gnōsis*) is not born with men, but is acquired, and the acquiring of it in its elements demands application, and training, and progress; and then from incessant practice it passes into a habit . . . ."[85] The contemplation of God is obviously the ultimate goal, which is the highest function of the soul. The sciences play an important role in the perfecting of the functions of the soul related to knowledge. There are no grapes without work in the vineyard, nor good results without a solid education, "[He] has learned to purpose, who has practiced the various lessons, so as to be able to cultivate and to heal. So also here, I call him truly learned who brings everything to bear on the truth; so that, from geometry, and music, and grammar, and philosophy itself, culling what is useful, he guards the faith against assault."[86] Clement devotes a lot of space to dialectic, which he places at the forefront of all these skills. He is also quite aware of the black legend with which the epoch of practical philosophy (wary as it was of speculation) surrounded dialectic. Clement defended dialectic with great determination, because he was aware of the value of dependable thinking for the emerging church. Even the episode where Jesus outsmarts the devil in the desert by pointing out the ambiguities of scripture provides an argument against those who think Satan is the

---

82. Ibid. VI.IX.74.1.

83. Ibid. II.XX.120.1, ANF 2, 373.

84. Hadot, *What is Ancient Philosophy?*, 241.

85. Clem. Al., *Str.* VI.IX.43.2–4, ANF 2, 498.

86. Ibid. I.IX.43.2–4, ANF 2, 309–10.

creator of philosophy and dialectic.[87] Clement considers the use of dialectic in the interpretation of the scriptures as fulfillment of "seek and you will find" (Matt 7:7). "Accordingly, by investigation, the point proposed for inquiry and answer knocks at the door of truth, according to what appears. And on an opening being made through the obstacle in the process of investigation, there results scientific contemplation."[88] The whole of Book VIII of the *Stromata* is devoted to logical puzzles, matters of proof (*apodeiksis*), syllogisms, distinctions, definitions, ambiguities, etc., which all turn out to be very important tools for the garden of faith.[89] After all, "authentic dialectic" is something more substantial than mere exercises for the mind, it is a path one climbs to reach toward God.[90]

While covering this path the gnostic extracts from each of these disciplines whatever will aid the proper functioning of reason. The unity of human nature means that it is not easy to separate the purely intellectual aspect of the exercises from their moral aspects. What is more, philosophical study helps in the study of the scriptures.[91] Music demonstrates the relations of harmonized sounds; arithmetic discovers numbers and their relations; geometry, while perfecting reason also helps it to tear itself away from the body, and it accommodates the intellectual grasping of the essence of immutable being; astronomy teaches how to go beyond the Earth; while dialectic distinguishes between beings and grasps first causes.[92] Clement's approach to the sciences does not differ from the approach of the philosophical schools. On the path to happiness nobody becomes totally absorbed by physics or astronomy in themselves. It is enough to recall Plato's *Timaeus*. The contemplation of harmony that reveals itself in the world of the senses thanks to astronomy or music should serve as an exercise in reaching inner harmony. Nothing is more foreign to the spirit of ancient philosophy than the notion of autonomous sciences and ethics. And so "it is necessary to avoid the great futility which occupies itself in irrelevant matters . . . ."[93] This is the reason why the gnostic should be on guard against confusing the passion for knowledge with spiritual exercises that lead to *gnōsis*, which is the fruit of a long and many-sided spiri-

---

87. Ibid. I.IX.44.4.

88. Ibid. VIII.I.1.3, ANF 2, 558.

89. Osborn considers this book to be an accidental insertion into the Miscellanies of a notebook from Clement's methodological readings. See: Osborn, *The Philosophy of Clement of Alexandria*, 149.

90. Clem. Al., *Str.* I.XXVIII.177.1—178.1.

91. Ibid. VII.XVI.95.9.

92. Ibid. VI.X.80.1–5.

93. Ibid. VI.X.82.4, ANF 2, 499.

tual practice and God's grace.[94] Only *gnōsis* leads to the desired contemplation of the Lord, step by step, until the highest perfection that can be attained in this bodily life, to a love that makes humanity a likeness of God.[95]

Faith is a germ of *gnōsis*, which consists of only the most essential news. Clement calls it, "a comprehensive knowledge of the essentials."[96] On the other hand, *gnōsis* is the certain, full, and indubitable knowledge of the presuppositions accepted by faith. The *gnōsis* built upon faith in the Lord's teaching, along with help from philosophy, conveys the soul "on to infallibility, science, and comprehension."[97] Let us not lose sight of the relationship this distinction has with the subjective understanding of knowledge about the most important things in life. On the purely objective side of things faith is not objectively any less true than *gnōsis*. The difference lies in faith being the state of mind of a person who is at the starting point of spiritual transformation. Faith is like an only partially proven hypothesis whose confirmation is reached at the end of moral and epistemological transformation, when, at its highest point, *gnōsis* transforms itself in to love. It is difficult to deny that in this way, "The philosophical notion of spiritual progress constitutes the very backbone of Christian education and teaching. As ancient philosophical discourse was for the philosophical way of life, so Christian philosophical discourse was a means of realizing the Christian way of life."[98]

Tertullian and the Roman Version of the Exercises

The argument that what Tertullian adopted for the needs of Christianity has many more elements of ancient philosophy than say, Justin Martyr, seems like it can be easily criticized, especially in light of the commonplace picture of Tertullian. We will attempt to defend precisely this argument while modifying the somewhat journalistic character of the judgment (what measure should we use to quantify the number of these elements?). What Tertullian took over from philosophy with the help of his immense intellectual talents and injected into the mainstream of Christian spirituality became so integrated with Christianity that it does not awaken suspicion even in the most suspicious despisers of un-Christian contamination.

94. Ibid. VI.X.82.1.
95. Ibid. VII.X.57.2.
96. Ibid. VII.X.57.3, ANF 2, 539.
97. Ibid.
98. Hadot, *What is Ancient Philosophy?*, 240.

The supposed absurdity of my argument can be mainly supported by the Carthaginian's well-known repulsion toward all forms of philosophical speculation, "We want no curious disputation after possessing Christ Jesus, no inquisition after enjoying the gospel! With our faith, we desire no further belief. For this is our palmary faith, that there is nothing which we ought to believe besides."[99] Attempts to justify speculation cannot lean upon Christ's words, "Seek and you will find" (Matt 7:7). These words, according to Tertullian, were directed to the Jews and pagans by God before the fullness of the truth was revealed, and so they find no application in reference to Christians.[100] Faith in Christ is the end of the searching, so it is impossible to search further without denying the faith through further searches.[101] There is no truth beyond God,[102] and it is even safer not to know than to transgress the boundaries of revelation in one's searches.[103] "Our instruction comes from 'the porch of Solomon,' who had himself taught that 'the Lord should be sought in simplicity of heart.' Away with all attempts to produce a mottled Christianity of Stoic, Platonic, and dialectic composition!"[104]

These uncompromising statements change their meaning somewhat when they are placed within the philosophical tradition from which they emerged and within the context where they were enunciated. When talking about these sources I would like to explain the process of adaptation of Greek philosophy by the Romans, a process that had its dramatic moments. On the other hand, we cannot overlook the context of Tertullian's polemic with the heterodox *gnōsis* that infiltrated Christianity.

The Romans and Philosophy

Quite a few things suggest Tertullian (a Latin) imposed the antinomy between faith and philosophical speculation upon the antinomy of Rome and Greece, and that the division between Jerusalem and Athens is undergrid by the division between the Empire and Athens. And so Tertullian inherits all the prejudices of brave soldiers, lawyers, and statesmen whose heads were all turned by philosophy.[105] The ambivalent relationship of the Romans to phi-

99. Tert., *Praescr.* 7, ANF 3, 246.

100. Ibid. 8.

101. Ibid. 9–12.

102. Tert., *An.* 1.4.

103. Ibid. 1.6.

104. Tert., *Praescr.* 7, ANF 3, 246.

105. Timothy David Barnes undermined the commonplace that Tertullian was educated in law in the book *Tertullian: A Historical and Literary Study*.

losophy, which combined an extreme revulsion and contempt (philosophy as a Hellenistic disease) with wonderment and adoration, can best serve as a reference point for understanding not only Tertullian's stance, but also the stances of many other Christians. This situation can be symbolized by the extravagantly eloquent scenery in Cicero's dialogue *On Moral Ends*, which presents the Latin reader with the central concepts of Greek philosophy. The philosophical discussion of Roman brilliance is staged within the Grove of Akademos. In order to understand the artistic power of Cicero's decision we must remember that just a few year earlier Sulla cut down trees from the grove for siege machines, which helped to defeat Athens.[106] Horace's claim that the military victors surrendered to the culture of the defeated Greeks was not an exaggeration.[107]

There are many different reasons why, in the Roman imagination, Greek philosophy usually occupies the same position traditionally reserved for sophistry. The roots of this idiosyncrasy can be gleaned in the shock registered in 154 BCE by the Romans after Carneades's envoy following Athenian aggression toward Oropus (an ally of Rome).

In two successive speeches Carneades amazed those gathered by first proving the reasonable (without exception) character of justice, only to later argue (not any less convincingly) for the kinship between justice and stupidity.[108] The most outstanding citizens of Rome, worried about the morale of the city's youth, forbade philosophy as a subject of study for several years after the infamous envoy.[109] Philosophy's later successes were always accompanied by suspicions of relativism, while careful Romans kept worrying whether the

106. See: Kumaniecki, *Cyceron i jego wspolczesni* [Cicero and His Contemporaries], 83.

107. "Graecia capta ferum victorem cepit et artes / intulit agresti Latio." Hor., *Ep.* II.1.156.

108. See: Cic., *Rep.* III; Lact., *Instit.* V.14.

109. See: Plin., *Hist. nat.* VII.30.112. While relating this episode Plutarch notes that Cato acknowledged there is a need to get rid of, "men who could easily convince them of anything they wanted. . . . This action was not motivated by dislike of Carneades, as some people believe, but by a general disapproval of philosophy and a desire to denigrate Greek culture and learning as a whole. After all, this is the man [Cato] who goes so far as to say that Socrates was a babbling bully who tried his utmost to set himself up as a tyrant . . . ." Plut., *Cat. Ma.* 22–23 [English translation: *Roman Lives*, 22–23, trans. Robin Waterfield, 30–31]. Earlier, in 173 BC, the senate expelled two Epicurean philosophers, Alkaios and Philiskos, and in 161 BC a measure was passed to ban all rhetoricians and philosophers. It speaks volumes that the same Cato, a politician and defender of the traditional morality under attack by the Greeks, known for his suspicion of everything that came from the nation of babblers, who saw Hellenization as an omen of his ruin, himself began to study Greek in his old age. See: Marrou, *Education in Antiquity*, 245–46.

rhetorical and logical exercises recommended by philosophy did not lose sight of the ultimate goals, that is, virtue and perfection.

Many of the questions about the role of philosophy in the lives of Roman citizens are similar to the ones asked by Christians.[110] Many of the stories told by Romans are reminiscent of those told by Christians. This even extends to the idea of Christianity as the realization of philosophy, since Cicero was convinced that only the Roman Empire realized the philosophical dreams of the Greeks.[111] The Romans would acknowledge philosophy as theirs in the sense that it found its crowning only, as they see it, in the perfection of Rome and the virtues of its heroes. Only in Rome did people finally become truly virtuous, only they knew the proper (effective) proportion of theory to practice, only in Rome did the harmony described by the Greeks reign, as was indirectly attested by the might of the Roman Empire, which was an earthly reflection of the cosmic order. In other words, Rome was the single greatest work of the mind.[112]

By the way, the identification of historical Rome with the realization of nature's perfection fell apart because of its restricted concept of *humanitas*, which uniformly labeled cultural phenomena not in agreement with those prevailing in Rome as against nature.[113] Furthermore, the Romans thought that the ideal of the citizen, when expressed in philosophical language, also makes the Roman the most proper way of life. Christians recognized the power of this way of thinking, this unique metaphysics of the Empire, when its prosecutors dragged them into the hands of executioners. This also explains why their apologies devoted so much attention to refuting this metaphysic by proving the immorality and injustice, that is, the unnaturalness of Rome.[114]

110. In the introduction to *On Moral Ends* Cicero writes: "Some people, by no means uneducated, altogether disapprove of philosophizing. Others do not criticize it so long as it is done in an easygoing manner, but consider that one should not devote so much of one's enthusiasm and attention to it." Cic., Fin. I.1.1. [English translation: Cicero, *On Moral Ends*, 3].

111. Cic., *Rep.* I.2.3.

112. Ibid. III.4.7. This was not only the opinion of the Empire's proponents. It is difficult to deny the tie between this ontology and the idea of the emperor's deification during the Principate. See: the very interesting observations on the theme of the Vergilian *Pax Augusta* as "the culmination of effort extending from the dawn of culture on the shores of the Mediterranean." Cochrane, *Christianity and Classical Culture*, 27.

113. Daniélou says the following about the misanthropy directed toward the Christians: "it expressed the fact that a community was suspect by reason of its peculiar customs. It was an easy jump from the idea of different customs to that of inhuman customs, since the Graeco-Roman civilisation was considered as the norm of *philanthropia*, of humanism." Daniélou and Marrou, *The First Six Hundred Years*, 82.

114. See: Min. Fel., *Oct.* 25.2–12; Tert., *Nat.* II.17.

But we should not forget when Tertullian speaks about philosophy, he not only speaks as a Christian purist, but also as a Roman citizen, suspicious of Greek tricks, which cannot but "produce no other effect than help to upset either the stomach or the brain."[115] Tertullian's critique of speculation exhibits ways of parodying the Greeks typical for the Romans, that is, by presenting philosophy as a pathologically pure form and, let us add, an inconclusive speculation. We should remember that we are looking at an epoch incapable of wresting itself from the choke-hold of skepticism, one that reduced philosophy to the contemplation of one's weaknesses. In response there was a call to substitute peripatetic living and paying lip-service to speculation with deeds in the writings of Plutarch, Seneca, Epictetus, and many others who saw in inconclusive controversies the decadence of a philosophy that abdicates its role as a teacher of life.[116]

In the first book of *On the Commonwealth* Cicero presents the difference between philosophy and politics (that is, Roman philosophy) precisely as the difference between pure contemplation and the active life, which is a harmonious combination of knowledge and right conduct. Philosophers are represented by Thales who never "looks at what's in front of his feet," yet, "they scan the tracts of the sky," while Scipio represents politics and combines cosmological knowledge with an impressive record of serving the state.[117] The Romans intended to use this argument, adopted by Tertullian, to point out the total divorce from real life of Greek thought, even though it claimed to be practical and a guide to life. Let us see what Tertullian said about Thales:

> Now, pray tell me, what wisdom is there in this hankering after conjectural speculations? What proof is afforded to us, notwithstanding the strong confidence of its assertions, by the useless affectation of a scrupulous curiosity, which is tricked out with an artful show of language? It therefore served Thales of Miletus quite right, when, star-gazing as he walked with all the eyes he had, he had the mortification of falling into a well, and was unmercifully twitted by an Egyptian, who said to him, "Is it because you found nothing on earth to look at, that you think you ought to confine your gaze to the sky?" His fall, therefore, is a figurative picture of the philosophers; of those, I mean, who persist in applying their studies to a vain purpose, since they indulge a stupid curiosity on

---

115. Tert., *Praescr.* 13, ANF 3, 251.

116. The most interesting attempt to break through this impasse is the concept of witness worked out simultaneously by the Christians and pagans.

117. Cic., *Rep.* I.18.30 [English translation: *On the Commonwealth and On the Laws*, trans. James E. G. Zetzel, 14].

natural objects, which they ought rather (intelligently to direct) to their Creator and Governor.[118]

It is important to remember that Tertullian stigmatizes useless precision and vain curiosity. Neither Tertullian nor the Romans reject reason. No, according to them, there is no more reasonable life than, respectively, either the Christian life, or that of a citizen of the Empire. In the work *On Penitence* Tertullian clearly underscores the tie between reason and God and the fact that only Christian knowledge about God allows one to live in harmony with the main driving force of reason, and therefore the actual order of a world that is ruled and pervaded by reason.[119] What is at stake is not reason in general, but reason in its proper function and the appropriate proportion between knowledge and action. We should not forget that what constitutes the appropriate proportions is determined by benefit, that is, effectiveness in putting one on the path toward salvation. What is authentically useful for man is at the same time good and in accordance with the will of God.[120] What Tertullian says in the *The Shows* can serve as a general principle; it is true that the world was created by God and it is good that God gave man dominion over it, but that does not mean that every manner of using the world is good. Natural knowledge about God's existence is not a sufficiently precise knowledge. But the pagans, "having no intimate acquaintance with the Highest, knowing Him only by natural revelation, and not as His 'friends'—afar off, and not as those who have been brought nigh to Him—men cannot but be in ignorance alike of what He enjoins and what He forbids in regard to the administration of His world."[121] The chasm between knowledge of the *ius naturale* and *ius familiare* is further conditioned by the deeds of Satan, the great parodist of God's intentions, who falsifies knowledge about the proper use of the created good.[122]

Only accurate knowledge about God permits one to properly understand the goal, function, and also the nature of the world, through the indirect help of philosophy. The overuse of reason is considered to be harmful, because it is unnatural and without purpose. When the gnostic of Clement of Alexandria, even though he is convinced of the factual inseparability of knowledge and utility (the good), chooses the good, Tertullian's Christian chooses obedience to God over utility. Tertullian even goes this far, "I hold it audacity to dispute about the 'good' of a divine precept; for, indeed, it is not the fact that it is good

---

118. Tert., *Nat.* II.4, ANF 3, 133.

119. Tert., *Paen.* 1.

120. Tert., *Ex.* 8.

121. Tert., *Spect.* 2, ANF 3, 80.

122. Ibid.

which binds us to obey, but the fact that God has enjoined it."[123] Reason has its limits and fully realizes its functions only by following the rule of faith. Its further progress, if it is at all possible and make sense, is closely tied to development through spiritual penalties and discipline, which solidify and develop both virtue and knowledge. The rule of faith, the Christian *credo*, which Tertullian brings up in the *Prescrption Against the Heretics*, is a sufficient depository of knowledge that is indispensable to a perfect and reasonable life.[124]

Actually, by sticking to this rule one can go further in one's research, in searching, in satisfying one's curiosity, in puzzling out unclear passages of the Bible; however, to put it indelicately, none of this is necessary. "You have acquired the knowledge of what you ought to know. 'Thy faith,' He says, 'hath saved thee'; not—observe—your skill in the Scriptures. Now, faith has been deposited in the rule; it has a law, and (in the observance thereof) salvation. Skill, however, consists in curious art, having for its glory simply the readiness that comes from knack. Let such curious art give place to faith; let such glory yield to salvation. At any rate, let them either relinquish their noisiness, or else be quiet. To know nothing in opposition to the rule (of faith), is to know all things (*Adversus regulam nihil scire omnia scire est*)."[125]

Heresy and the Treatment of Hellenic Illnesses

We would be committing an inexcusable mistake thinking that the passages we quoted above discredit the need to use any philosophy at all. Pierre Hadot points out that the majority, if not all, of the ancient philosophical texts refer to the concrete spiritual condition of their readers, to a human being upon a specific stage of spiritual development, oftentimes they help him to overcome a particular type of spiritual illness. Since there is no universal cure for each and every ailment of the soul then one should not approach ancient texts, without the risk of uncovering only apparent contradictions, by taking them out of their immediate context of addressing a specific illness.[126] This applies to

123. Tert., *Paen.* 4, ANF 3, 660.

124. Tert., *Praescr.* 13.

125. Ibid. 14, ANF 3, 250 (with some modifications).

126. "Whether we have to do with dialogues as in the case of Plato, class notes as in the case of Aristotle, treatises like those of Plotinus, or commentaries like those of Proclus, a philosopher's work cannot be interpreted without taking into consideration the concrete situation which gave birth to them. They are the products of a philosophical school, in the most concrete sense of the term, in which a master forms his disciples, trying to guide them to self-transformation and realization. Thus, the written work is a reflection of pedagogical, psychagogic, and methodological preoccupations. Although

Tertullian more than to any other thinker. Of course, just like every physician, he did have his own definition of health, however, every instance of spiritual illness is a separate mystery for him. We will return to his ideal of perfection and demonstrate how many different philosophical exercises he considered to be applicable on the philosophical way. For now we will turn our attention toward the situation that brought about the *Prescription Against the Heretics*.

Much like the majority of ancient philosophers, Tertullian does not devise a doctrine, instead he fosters a spiritual transformation without losing time preaching to the choir. Like the Platonic Socrates, who addresses Calicles differently than he does Euthyphro, and Parmenides altogether differently, Tertullian adjusts his own discourse to the personal needs of his hearer. He does not speak to the alcoholic about the benefits of alcohol, nor does he tell the coward about caution. Saint Jerome agrees with this universal precept about the nature of a moral education: "there is no greater folly than to teach a pupil what he knows already."[127] In a *Prescription* addressed to Christians tempted by heresy there is no reason to prove the philosophical nature of revelation because the audience of the treatise most likely does not suffer from a deficit of enthusiasm for speculation. The problem, as Tertullian sees it, has to do with the integral nature of revelation and the dangers posed to it by Hellenic wisdom.[128] The gnostic interpretations of Christianity, with their heavy reliance upon the philosophical-religious culture of Hellenism, are enough to question the value of philosophy.[129] The fathers accused philosophy of being

---

every written work is a monologue, the philosophical work is always implicitly a dialogue. The dimension of the possible interlocutor is always present within it. This explains the incoherencies and contradictions which modern historians discover with astonishment in the works of ancient philosophers. In philosophical works such as these, thought cannot be expressed according to the pure, absolute necessity of a systematic order. Rather, it must take into account the level of the interlocutor, and the concrete tempo of the logos in which it is expressed." Hadot, *Philosophy as a Way of Life*, 104–5.

127. Hier., *Epist.* 22.27, NPNF 2, 33.

128. Worries about the influence of this type of religiosity are not reserved solely for Christians. There is also an analogy with the worries of some Romans. Cochrane says in *Christianity and Classical Culture*, 2–3, "The Pantheon was crowded to the point of suffocation by a host of extraneous deities. Powerful court circles listened with attention to the ravings of Asiatic theosophists. The vogue of astrology was such as to draw forth the condemnation of successive emperors, culminating in the fiery denunciation of Diocletian, 'the whole damnable art of the mathematici is forbidden' (*tota damnabilis ars mathematica interdicta est*)."

129. Above all, we must always remember that even here we are dealing with an instance of opposition to philosophy, not an opposition to reason. Henry Chadwick writes, "So, although the short-term effect of gnostic propaganda was to make many believers fearful of philosophical speculations, it remains true to say that the Church rejected the

the mother of all heresies, because they were worried about unity of doctrine, which was being blown up by gnostic criticisms of the Bible, and gnostic syncretism and theological speculations.[130] What was at stake is how heterodox *gnōsis* willingly uses philosophy and revelation as the basis for its abstruse and fairy-tale theogonies.[131] The philosophical aspirations of some gnostics (independently of their quality) are reminiscent of the transformation of the multiplicity of philosophical schools into a multiplicity of sects falsifying the deposit of faith. According to Tertullian, the Platonist Valentinus derived his teaching on *aeōns* from philosophy, and the Stoic-inspired Marcion got his teaching about two gods from the same source. While those who believe the soul is mortal follow Epicurus and those who imagine God as a fire follow Heraclitus. Those who deny the resurrection of the body merely rehash the arguments of all previous philosophical schools.[132] For example, Aristotelian dialectic is especially dangerous, "Unhappy Aristotle! who invented for these men dialectics, the art of building up and pulling down; an art so evasive in its propositions, so far-fetched in its conjectures, so harsh in its arguments, so productive of contentions—embarrassing even to itself, retracting everything, and really treating of nothing!"[133]

It is easy to understanding how this was a context where the praise of speculation did not seem like the most pressing matter. *Gnōsis* constitutes for Tertullian an example of an activity of the intellect that is given over to the

---

Gnostics because they used reason too little rather than because they used it too much. For in rejecting the gnostic way the Christians thereby rejected as an inauthentic adulteration and corruption any theology of pure revelation teaching salvation by an arbitrary predestination of the elect and the total depravity of the lost, and possessing no criteria of rational judgment. In any event, the Church could not escape reasoned argument if it was ever to explain itself and so extend its missions to world." Chadwick, *Early Christian Thought and the Classical Tradition*, 9.

130. See: Tert., *Prescr.* 7; Ap. 47.9. None of this has to be associated with completely ruling out the value of philosophy. For example, Hippolytus stresses how philosophy stands higher than its gnostic parodies: "We must not overlook any figment devised by those denominated philosophers among the Greeks. For even their incoherent tenets must be received as worthy of credit, on account of the excessive madness of the heretics; who, from the observance of silence, and from concealing their own ineffable mysteries, have by many been supposed worshipers of God" (*Ref.* 1, ANF 5, 9).

131. For ancient Gnosticism, see: Daniélou and Marrou, *The First Six Hundred Years*, 55–61; Quispel, *Gnostica, Judaica, and Catholica*; Jonas, *The Gnostic Religion*; Michalski, *Antologia Literatury Patrystycznej*, 145–51; Myszor, "Introduction" to *Teksty z Nag-Hammadi* [Texts from Nag-Hammadi], 11–100, which is devoted to the Valentinians and the library in Nag-Hammadi.

132. Tert., *Praescr.* 7.

133. Ibid. 7, ANF 3, 246.

passions of pride, curiosity, and the lust for fame; it has become independent of the real needs of humanity. Pride leads people astray and tends to lead to the worship of false gods. Apostasy, like false philosophy, is therefore the work and worship of Satan.[134] Heresy becomes a carnal sin,[135] because living in a lie must lead to immorality.[136] The situation is further intensified by the fact that some of the gnostic sects, as if they were embodying the Roman caricatures of philosophy, actually did limit themselves to theory or knowledge exclusively (*gnōsis*), while totally ignoring the demands of a moral life.[137] Even though this immoral variation on salvation (through *gnōsis* alone) was not very common it only furthers the impulse to suspect various forms of speculation. When we talk about Tertullian it helps to remember the bitter critique of *gnōsis* we find in Plotinus. A reading of the *Enneads* is the best proof that the gnostic indifference toward ethical questions repulsed more than just Roman Christians who were overly cautious about excessive flights of the spirit.[138]

The Adaptation of Spiritual Exercises

Tertullian was ruthless toward philosophy wherever it misappropriated the deposit of faith, but he also willingly resorted to it wherever useful. Let us stress that this is not a problem of a lack of consequence, or a lack of understanding, but a problem of finding the right procedures for addressing specific situations. It is not that the end sanctifies the means, it is that there are no useless remedies if we know their ends and are able to apply them in the right situation, dose, and time. When addressing zealous intellectuals, who cannot see the possibility of salvation without dialectic, Tertullian says mischievously that Christ probably made a mistake sending simple fishermen to teach the gospel, not sophists; he obviously does not mean that all Christians are fishermen.[139] This then is the reason why (not out of inconsequentiality) the famed anti-rationalist does not shy away from employing philosophy for

134. Ibid. 40.

135. Ibid. 6.

136. Ibid. 41.

137. On gnostic nihilism or libertinism see: Jonas, *The Gnostic Religion*, 320–41; Daniélou and Marrou, *The First Six Hundred Years*, 59–61.

138. See: Hadot, *Plotinus or the Simplicity of Vision*, 66–67. See: the ironic observations of Clement of Alexandria about a gnostic immoralist who attempted to overcome pleasures by practicing them, or the debauchery of the Nicolaitians in *Str.* II.XX.117.4—118.6; III.IV.25.7—29.1; on the libertinism of the followers of Prodicos (a sect of antinomians) see: Ibid. III.IV.30.1–3.

139. Tert., *An.* 3.3.

the work of salvation, in practice agreeing with the Romans that it is possible to philosophize, so long as one does it in the proper measure.[140]

Tertullian's picture of this proper measure owes a lot to Roman Stoicism and Academicism and their pictures of humanity's perfection. Just like in Clement it is connected to the picture of the inner harmony of God's image, which is given to humanity, thereby regaining the state of nature destroyed by the Tempter.[141] Much like in all of ancient philosophy, the complete spiritual-bodily transformation is simultaneously a rejection and a return. However, the role reason plays is different than in Clement. It finds its limits not in contemplating God, but in a specific self-limitation of the intellectual passions which Tertullian sees as the spiritual equivalent of the body's passions.[142] Anyway, the deeds of the spirit and the body cannot be separated at all, because "it is not the fact that body and spirit are two things that constitute the sins mutually different—otherwise they are on this account rather *equal*, because the *two* make up *one*. . . . The *guilt* of both is common; common, too, is the *Judge*—God to wit; common, therefore, is withal the healing medicine of repentance."[143] The Christian situation is unique because Christians have received the whole truth from God. This does not mean, of course, that anyone who has read the Bible is already perfect. The development of knowledge is accompanied by a spiritual transformation and is expressed in the development of virtue that manifests itself in progress in spiritual discipline.[144] Its peak is intimate knowledge of God, which is a type of likeness to God.[145]

The succeeding stages of spiritual progress demand a series of exercises with a decidedly spiritual provenance. Tertullian did not write a systematic work covering all the useful spiritual exercises, however, his timely interventions allow us to create a clear picture of this matter. A part of his intellectual exercises is connected with, it seems, mostly the introductory stages of the spiritual path and finds its application among people who have something like a philosophical formation. On the one hand, they teach what place the testimony of the soul or the cosmological argument have in revealing the rational character of revelation. On the other hand, as we saw in Tertullian's

---

140. See: Cic., *Rep.* I.18.30.

141. Tert., *Spect.* 2.

142. But this does not mean contemplation is totally exiled from Tertullian's world. See: Tert., *Mart.* 2.

143. Tert., *Paen.* 3, ANF 3, 658–59.

144. Tert., *Praescr.* 43–44.

145. Tert., *Spect.* 2.

attack upon dialectic,[146] or in his critique of pagan theology,[147] the aim of some of the exercises is to demonstrate and consolidate a conviction about the ineffectiveness of reason alone, an ineffectiveness that expresses itself in the contradictions of philosophy that cannot be resolved through rational philosophical judgments. While Tertullian leans upon Stoic experience to deal with the first set of problems, in his response to the second he is indebted to skeptical attacks upon dogmatic philosophy—as demonstrated in the speech of Carneades, and part of standard academic exercises, namely, the proofs of the isosthenia of philosophical judgments.

When we free ourselves from thinking about ancient philosophy in purely doctrinal categories (which can only point us to Tertullian's debt to Stoic materialism, or, for example, toward the concept of the law) we discover a series of techniques of spiritual conversion, which Tertullian (like Clement) permanently introduced into Christianity. In Tertullian we can find all the Stoic-Platonic exercises mentioned by Philo of Alexandria. For example: study, meditation (*meletai*), cures for the passions (*therapeiai*), recalling the beautiful, self-control, doing one's duties,[148] or others, such as: listening with a constant attention that is turned upon oneself (*prosochē*)[149] and indifference toward indifferent things. There was no lack of typical Cynical exercises to combat the passions through bodily mortification. These exercises became so rooted in Christian spirituality that our contemporaries are surprised to discover the ancient philosophical roots of Tertullian's advice to meditate upon the Lord's Prayer by first purifying oneself of anger or an unquiet heart.[150] One can confidently say that for Tertullian constant spiritual exercises constitute the content of daily life for members of Christ's church. Tertullian underscores this fact in his description of the Christian life by willingly and frequently resorting to military-athletic metaphors that were also favorites of the philosophers. The sustained fight with the passions Satan fuels, a constant readiness to battle, concentration of thoughts upon fighting the enemy, working upon spiritual and bodily conditioning, the stubborn taking up anew of the difficulties of the exercises, and severe penalties are the content of many memorable and striking examples for readers.[151]

The unity of the bodily-spiritual human nature means that it is difficult to divide up the exercises into the spiritual and the moral. It is evident that

146. Tert., *Praescr.* 7.

147. Tert., *Nat.* II.2–17.

148. Phil. Al., *Leg. alleg.* III.18.

149. Hadot, *Philosophy as a Way of Life*, 82–89.

150. Tert., *Or.* 11–12.

151. See: The suggestive metaphor of believers as *militia Christi* in Tert., *Mart.* 3.

all of them aim at sustaining a complete spiritual conversion. The exercises already begin before baptism. Tertullian chastises the catechumens who do not pursue an appropriate spiritual disposition that is reinforced by penance.

"Not that I deny that the divine benefit," says Tertullian, "—the putting away of sins, I mean—is in every way sure to such as are on the point of entering the (baptismal) water; but what we have to labour for it, that it may be granted us to attain that blessing."[152] The consolidation of a spiritual disposition is the meaning of all the spiritual exercises, and as this gives priority to God who becomes known in the process, it also completely restructures the believer's life around him.[153] Tertullian's Christian constantly thinks about God, recalling the sayings of the prophets, or deepening his understanding of the Psalms, much like members of philosophical schools of the time whose spiritual work, above all, revolved around the study of foundational texts.[154] Daily prayer was for him an opportunity for moral self-knowledge (*gnōthi seauton!*): "A petition for pardon is a full confession; because he who begs for pardon fully admits his guilt."[155] The transformation engages the whole person, not only the reason and the will, but also the imagination. This is also why in the fight against the passions Tertullian, like the ancients, engages the full arsenal of means. For example, rhetorical amplifications play a significant role. There is the Stoic *premeditatio malorum* (meditation upon unavoidable misfortunes, which in the end are insignificant for the philosopher) that is supposed to help against the fluctuations of fate, just as meditating upon oppressive images of remaining in the clutches of the passions and their dark eschatological consequences help to subjugate the passions.[156] Some spiritual exercises need to be practiced alone, whereas others require the supervision of an expert.[157] Thus, a teacher who has the grace of biblical knowledge should help in the study of the Bible.[158] As an expert in the spiritual exercises Tertullian cares about equipping Christians in clear and simple formulas helpful in any situation. This is the source of the Carthaginian's aphoristic style, the quotable sentences and concise formulations, and it is also why he uses the rule of faith in much the same way as the Stoics or Epicureans used simple

---

152. Tert., *Paen.* 6, ANF 3, 661.

153. Ibid. 5.

154. See: Tert., *Spect.* 25; Pierre Hadot, *What is Ancient Philosophy?*, 239.

155. Tert., *Or.* 7, ANF 3, 684.

156. Tert., *Spect.* 30.

157. Tert., *Or.* 1.

158. Tert., *Praescr.* 14.

dogmatic formulas in their teaching.[159] Tertullian's treatise *On Patience*, by its very name, is connected with the Stoic tradition of treatise-long exercises, such as: *On Anger, On Curiosity*, or *On Overcoming the Passions*, which issued from the pens of Seneca or Plutarch.

However, transformation does not automatically sustain itself, only death definitively closes the period of earthly travail. This is why even a free man cannot discontinue the exercises. It is also the reason why even people close to perfection succumb to the passions, overcome by human traditions they abandon the rule of faith,[160] they abandon themselves to earthly temptations, and surrender their spirit to the reign of bodily lusts.[161] In the so-called "second repentance" permitted by Tertullian we see a synthetic image of the return to God and escape from these passions. Confession,[162] the acknowledgment of faults, which teaches about moral weakness and the goodness of God; bodily mortification, which are a form of a radical curtailing of the passions; meditation upon the wickedness of committed sins, which sustains conviction about proper order, and prayer[163] are all bodily *and* spiritual medicines, which should not be recommended only to backsliders.[164]

As we can see, for Tertullian the degree of one's spiritual development is also dependent upon exercises whose philosophical origins do not change the fact that the Carthaginian considers them an integral component of Christian life. Both his Roman formation and fear of heresy meant that Tertullian not only less willingly acknowledged his debts (than, for example, Clement), he also called Christianity a philosophy much less frequently than his Greek contemporaries. Like the heroes of Cicero, who prefer talking about Roman politics to talking about philosophy, Tertullian, agrees to the obvious similarities, but he emphasizes the superiority of God's work over human philosophy.[165] However, when Tertullian takes Plato down a notch for thinking that God is difficult to find, and proposes any old Christian artisan who already has found God and proves his knowledge through his deeds, we know that the life of this

159. See: Hadot, *Philosophy as a Way of Life*, 82–89.

160. Tert., *Praescr.* 3.

161. Tert., *Paen.* 8.

162. The examination of conscience belongs to exercises recommended by the Pythagorean school (See: *DL* VIII.22), much like the practice of poverty, silence, which was so admired by Clement (*Str.* V.XI.67.3), and moderation (*DL* VIII.10).

163. Tert., *Paen.* 9.

164. Ibid. 12.

165. Tert., *Ap.* XLVI.2–3.

artisan is filled with exercises well-known to the philosophers condemned by the Carthaginian.[166]

166. Ibid. XLVI.9; See: Iust., *Apol.* II.10.8; Min. Fel., *Oct.* 16.6.

Conclusion

SATAN HAS NOT STOLEN our world from under our noses. The world was not created by an evil demon. Even if it seems to be broken, Genesis demands we remember it was created "good" by God. The Christians (unlike those who succumb to Manichean temptations) cannot simply wipe out the world, which obviously does not mean the world is perfect, because, after all, a disposition toward the good and its actualization are two different things. Even if the world contains so much luster, even if it promises a compromise, we should still not forget that we are in conflict with it. The conflict is one of life and death. We can admire the world, learn about it, we can use it, but we should know its dangers, and that it needs to be saved. Above all: the world needs to be saved!

This is what the Apologists can teach us about the world, culture, and philosophy. Their pendulum steadily swings between contempt and wonder. The aim is not compromise between these stances, rather we need both the extremes of the swing simultaneously. Each extreme taken on its own is too confined for Christian teaching, and so: neither unconditional rejection, nor unconditional embrace. After all, we are on the way like Odysseus to Ithaca. We find ourselves here for a short moment, being here is like finding ourselves strangers in a strange land. As guests and passersby we must take care of what has been entrusted to us; we should use it sensibly, but we should not make ourselves too much at home, because we ought not forget where we are heading.

If we are on the way, said Augustine many years after the Apologists in his treatise *De doctrina christiana*, if we are wayfarers who want to return home, then we must see the world as a means of transportation (*terestibus vel marinis vehiculis*) and always remember to distinguish the means and ends. The metaphor of returning home serves to demonstrate the order of goods and so the right attitude toward earthly goods. Augustine enjoyed this homely comparison greatly. It served him during his youth (when he was a Marinist[1]) as an image of the path to happiness. In his maturity it returned as an

---

1. See: *De vita beata* I.1–5.

image of the path to salvation, "So in this mortal life we are like travelers away from our Lord [2 Cor 5:6]: if we wish to return to the homeland where we can be happy we must use (*utendum*) this world, not enjoy (*fruendum*) it . . . ."[2]

The Latin *uti* and *frui* are not easily translated into English or other modern languages without losing their meaning.[3] In the hierarchical world of Augustine the formula *uti-frui* allows us to distinguish three categories of being. The first category is composed of what we must feast upon (*frui*), rejoice over, when we possess it, or rather our clinging to it (how helpless language is here!) makes us happy. This is the Truine God.[4] The second category is composed of all those things that aid in the attainment of the goods that make us happy. The work of philosophy is surely among them. The third category is composed of beings somewhere between those of the previous categories. They are not ultimate ends, but they reward us with a happiness that is a foretaste of perfection, they are a signal that we are headed in the right direction[5] (another human being is such a good, when we can rejoice about them in God and when they direct us toward God. We ourselves are such a good and so are the holy angels).[6] This obviously is the proper order of love. When it reigns within a human it becomes the capacity to love things in proportion to their good.[7] This is the love that sets us free.[8]

The metaphor of a "means of transportation" helps to reveal the absurdity of giving autonomy to particular instruments, the ineptness of exchanging means for ends. Augustine writes, "but if we choose to enjoy things that are to be used, our advance is impeded and sometimes even diverted, and we are

---

2. Augustinus, *De doctrina christiana* I.IV.4 [English translation: *On Christian Teaching*, trans. R. H. Green, 10].

3. See: Domański, *Z dawnych rozważań o marności i pogardzie świata* [From Ancient Considerations of the Wretchedness and Hatred of the World and the Poverty and Dignity of Man], 7–12.

4. Augustinus, *De doctrina christiana* I.V.5; I.VI.6; See also: *De doctrina christiana*, 10: "Have I spoken something, have I uttered something worth of God? No, I feel that all I have done is to wish to speak; if I did say something, it is not what I wanted to say".

5. Ibid. I.III.3.

6. Ibid. I.XXII.20–21; I.XXX.31–33; I.XXIII.22; I.XXXIII.37. The intermediate state between *uti* and *frui* is *uti cum delectatione*.

7. Ibid. I.XXIII.22; I.XXVII.28; I.XXIX.30; I.XXX.33.

8. The universality of love and possibility: what to do with the obvious fact that, "all people should be loved equally," when it founders against the realities of the human condition, upon the limitations imposed upon our love by space and time ("But you cannot do good to all people equally" [*omnibus prodesse non possis*])? One ought to help those whom circumstances have tied to us most closely. See: Ibid. I.XXVIII.29, 21.

held back, even put off, from attaining things which are to be enjoyed . . . ."[9] In relation to philosophy, the wonderfully flexible formula *uti-frui* confirms the teaching of the Apologists. These concepts are crucial for analyzing Greek wisdom and practice, in its capacity to help us die to the world and liken ourselves to the truth. Philosophy as a goal in itself and for itself can only lead to death.[10]

This is an important element of the legacy left behind by the fathers. It can be observed in their openness, which is not naive. These are people who only read the Bible on their knees. They are aware of the similarities, but they can see the differences, and they are not afraid to clearly define the boundaries of orthodoxy and the boundaries of inquiry. They are brave in entering the dispute, but, above all, they are courageous—this is difficult to define, but it is obviously noticeable upon every page written by them—they do not retreat into the catacombs. They possess the boldness and aggressiveness of people who through imitating their Lord want to transform their world. They neither want to justify it, nor do they want to condemn it—they want to save it.

The latter tradition also confirmed the distaste of the Apologists for fideism. Both the Augustinian "faith seeking understanding," and the philosophy of Aquinas grow out of the perspective of the fathers with regard to this matter. Mind you, this is not some linguistic manipulation, which confuses contemporary philosophical standards with rationality. What is at stake is an attempt to measure up to the task laid down for philosophy by academic skepticism. It is a difficult trial, which from the start eliminates the pre-Pyrrhic dogmatic naivete as an option for Christian philosophy. The Apologists take up this task going arm in arm with the representatives of philosophical schools, and they willingly borrow their best achievements.

The following are the most important fruits of these undertakings: the cosmological argument, Tertullian's testimony of the soul, the *apodeiksis* of the witnesses, Justin's doctrine of the *Logos*, the original understanding of *pistis* as the initial axiom for a systematic knowledge of God. They cannot be circumvented, no matter what we think of them. It is also impossible, without using anachronistic criteria, to place them safely within the confines of faith, or place them in opposition to the philosophical standards of the time. The stance of the Apologists on reason is one of the most important stories in the testimony they leave behind. This testimony excluded from the very beginning gnostic fables from the Christian heritage and it fused the question of reason with the living tradition of the church permanently. Christian philosophy discovered its tone in the controversies against Pyrrhonism and fideism. It did not change its principles, but it learned its lessons. Pyrrhonism became

9. Ibid. I.III.3, 9.
10. Ibid. I.XX.19.

a vaccine of humility against the dogmatic naivete of reason, while gnosticism became a warning against faith celebrating its irrationality.

The last crucial matter in the testimony of the Apologists taken over from philosophy—or more precisely, developed thanks to it—is the idea of spiritual development and the spiritual exercises. The *Execrcitia spiritualia* of Ignatius of Loyola best confirm the lasting connection between Christian spirituality with ancient philosophical *ascesis*.[11] There is no need to describe the further history of this connection in order to imagine how different Christian life would be if we were to deprive it of the techniques of spiritual conversion it borrowed from philosophy.[12] Of course there are difficulties in adopting this tradition. One of them is the holiness of ordinary believers, not only of interest to Clement's gnostic,[13] but also for Tertullian's artisan who has ordered his life with a severe discipline of philosophical exercises. We have already discussed the problems associated with intellectual and/or ascetic elitism. We should remind ourselves that individual spiritual work invites Pelagianism into the church through the back door, which ends up questioning the meaning and need for the sacrifice of Christ. The teaching on grace is the cure for both ascetic elitism and for Pelagianism. We should remember how the elderly man put emphasis upon this teaching in his conversation with Justin the Platonist. This emphasis did not let up over time. It became the topic of great controversies and schisms. The balance sheet between the necessity of spiritual effort and the consciousness of how evanescent our efforts are will no doubt remain one of the most important traits of the spiritual culture of the Christian world.

11. See: Rabbow, *Methodik der Exerzitien in der Antike*.

12. On the Christian history of the spiritual exercises see: Hadot, "Ancient Philosophical Exercises and 'Christian Philosophy'" in *Philosophy as a Way of Life*, 126–44.

13. On the varieties of Christian piety see: Clem. Al., *Str.* IV.XXI.133.1.

Bibliography

Alighieri, Dante. *The Divine Comedy: Hell*. Translated by Henry Wadsworth Longfellow. London: Routledge, 1867.

Armstrong, A. H., and R. A. Markus. *Christian Faith and Greek Philosophy*. London: Darton, Longman & Todd, 1960.

Augustine. *City of God Against the Pagans*. Translated by R. W. Dyson. Cambridge: Cambridge University Press, 1998.

———. *On Christian Teaching*. Translated by R. H. Green. Oxford: Oxford University Press, 2008.

Barnes, Timothy David. *Tertullian: A Historical and Literary Study*. Oxford: Clarendon, 1971.

Burkert, Walter. *The Orientalizing Revolution: Near Eastern Influence on Greek Culture in the Early Archaic Age*. Translated by Margaret Pinder. Cambridge: Harvard University Press, 1997.

Butterworth, G. W. "The Deification of Man in Clement of Alexandria." *Journal of Theological Studies* 17 (1916) 157–69.

Chadwick, Henry, *Early Christian Thought and the Classical Tradition*. Oxford: Oxford University Press, 1984.

———. *History and Thought of Early Church*. London: Variorum Reprint, 1982.

———. "Philo and the Beginning of Christian Thought." In *The Cambridge History of Later Greek and Early Medieval Philosophy*, edited by Arthur Hilary Armstrong, 137–57. Cambridge: Cambridge University Press, 1967.

Cicero. *The Nature of the Gods*. Translated by Horace Cecil Pancras McGregor. New York: Penguin Classics, 1972.

———. *On the Commonwealth and On the Laws*. Translated by James E. G. Zetzel. Cambridge: Cambridge University Press, 1999.

———. *On Moral Ends*. Translated by Raphael Woolf. Cambridge: Cambridge University Press, 2001.

Cochrane, Charles Norris. *Christianity and Classical Culture*. Oxford: Oxford University Press, 1957.

Colisch, Marcia L. *The Stoic Tradition from Antiquity to the Early Middle Ages*, Vol. 2: *Stoicism in Christian Latin Thought through the Sixth Century*. New York: Krill, 1990.

Daniélou, Jean. *Gospel Message and Hellenistic Culture*. Translated by John Austin Baker. London: Darton, Longman &Todd, 1973.

Daniélou Jean, and Marrou Henri-Irenee. *The First Six Hundred Years*. Translated by Vincent Cronin. London: Darton, Longman, Todd, 1964.

Deman Thomas. *Chrystus Pan i Sokrates* [Christ the Lord and Socrates]. Translated by Zofia Starowieyska-Morstinowa. Warsaw: PAX, 1953.

Dembińska-Siury, Dobrochna. "Filozoficzne duszpasterstwo: O religijnej misji Sokratesa" [Philosophical Priesthood: The Religious Mission of Socrates]. In *Teologia Polityczna* [Political Theology] 2 (2004–5) 208–18.

Domański, Juliusz. *Erazm i filozofia. Studium o koncepcji filozofii Erazma z Rotterdamu* [Erasmus and Philosophy: A Study on Erasmus of Rotterdam's Conception of Philosophy]. Wrocław: Zakład Narodowy im. Ossolińskich, 1973.

———. *Metamorfozy pojęcia filozofii* [Metamorphoses in Understandings of Philosophy]. Translated by Z. Mroczkowska, Monika Bujko. In Renesans i Reformacja. Studia z Historii Filozofii i Idei [Renaissance and Reformation: Studies from the History of Philosophy and Ideas], edited by Lech Szczucki. Warsaw: Instytut Filozofii i Socjologii PAN, 1996.

———. "Quelques observations sur l'attitude d'Erasme envers la philosophie" [Some Observations on the Attitude of Erasmus towards Philosophy]. *Neohelicon* 1–2 (1975) 87–102.

———. "Patrystyczne postawy wobec dziedzictwa antycznego" [Patristic Stands toward the Heritage of Antiquity]. In *Idea: Studia nad strukturą i rozwojem pojęć* [Idea: Studies on the Structure and Development of Concepts] 5 (1992) 16–67.

———. "«Scholastyczne» i «humanistyczne» pojęcie filozofii" [The "Scholastic" and "Humanist" Conceptions of Philosophy]. In *Studia Mediewistyczne* [Medieval Studies] 1 (1978) 8–24.

———. *Z dawnych rozważań o marności i pogardzie świata oraz o nędzy i godności człowieka* [From Ancient Considerations of the Wretchedness and Hatred of the World and the Poverty and Dignity of Man]. Warsaw: Polska Akademia Nauk, 1997.

Dzielska, Maria. "Wstęp" [Introduction] to Proclus, *Elementy Teologii* [The Elements of Theology]. Translated by Robert Sawa. Warsaw: Wydawnictwo Akme, 2002.

Edwards M. J. "On the Platonic Schooling of Justin Martyr." *The Journal of Theological Studies* 42 (1991) 17–34.

Giles, J. A. *The Writings of the Early Christians of the Second Century.* Translated by J. A. Giles. Charleston: Nabu, 2010.

Gilson, Étienne. *Heloise and Abelard.* Ann Arbor, MI: University of Michigan Press, 1960.

———. *Historia filozofii chrześcijańskiej w wiekach średnich* [History of Christian Philosophy in the Middle Ages]. Translated by Sylwester Zalewski. Warsaw: PAX, 1987.

———. *The Spirit of Medieval Philosophy.* South Bend, IN: Notre Dame, 1991.

Hadot, Ilsetraut. "The Spiritual Guide." In *Classical Mediterranean Spirituality,* edited by Arthur Hilary Armstrong, 436–52. London: Routledge, 1986.

Hadot, Pierre. *The Inner Citadel: The Meditations of Marcus Aurelius.* Translated by Michael Chase. Cambridge: Harvard University Press, 2001.

———. *Philosophy as a Way of Life.* Oxford: Blackwell, 1995.

———. *Plotinus or the Simplicity of Vision.* Translated by Michael Chase. Chicago: University of Chicago Press, 1998.

———. *What is Ancient Philosophy?* Cambridge: Harvard University Press, 2002.

Harnack, Adolf. *History of Dogma,* Vol. 1. Translated by Neil Buchanan. London: Williams & Norgate, 1894.

———. *History of Dogma,* Vol. 2. Translated by Neil Buchanan. Boston: Little, Brown, and Company, 1907.

————. "Sokrates und die Alte Kirche" [Socrates and the Old Church]. In *Reden und Aufsatze* [Speeches and Essays], Vol. 1. Giessen: Ricker, 1906.

————. *What is Christianity?* Translated by T. B. Sounders. New York: Putnam's Sons, 1902.

Herodotus. *The Histories: Revised.* Translated by Aubrey de Selincourt. New York: Penguin, 2003.

Holte, Ragnar. "Logos Spermatikos. Christianity and Ancient Philosophy according to St. Justin's Apologies." *Studia Theologica* 12 (1958) 268–70.

Jaeger, Werner. *Early Christianity and Greek Paideia.* Cambridge: Belknap, 1961.

Jonas, Hans. *The Gnostic Religion.* Boston: Beacon, 2000.

Jung, Carl Gustav. *Psychological Types.* Translated by H. G. Baynes. Princeton: Princeton University Press, 1976.

Kaczmarkowski, Michał. "Językoznawstwo w *Kratylosie* Platona" [Linguistics in Plato's *Cratylus*]. In Platon [Plato], *Kratylos* [Cratylus], translated by Zofia Brzostowska. Lublin, Poland: KUL, 1990.

Karłowicz, Dariusz. *Arcyparadoks śmierci: O dowodowej wartości męczeństwa* [The Archparadox of Death: Martyrdom as a Philosophical Category]. Kraków: Znak 2000.

Kelly, John N. D. *Early Christian Doctrines.* New York: Continuum, 2005.

Kierkegaard Søren. *Fear and Trembling.* Translated by Alastair Hannay. New York: Penguin, 1985.

Kołakowski, Leszek. *Religion: If There Is No God.* South Bend, IN: St. Augustine's Press, 2001.

Kumaniecki, Kazimierz. *Cyceron i jego współcześni* [Cicero and His Contemporaries]. Warsaw: Czytelnik 1989.

Lilla, Salvatore. *Clement of Alexandria: A Study in Christian Platonism and Gnosticism.* Oxford: Oxford University Press, 1971.

Lucian. *Selected Satires of Lucian.* Translated by Lionel Casson. New York: Norton, 1968.

Newman, John Henry. *On the Development of Christian Doctrine.* South Bend, IN: University of Notre Dame Press, 1990.

Marrou, Henri-Irenee. *Education in Antiquity.* Madison, WI: University of Wisconsin Press, 1956.

Meeks, Wayne A. *The Origins of Christian Morality.* Translated by George Lamb. New Haven: Yale University Press, 1993.

Michalski, Marian, ed. *Antologia Literatury Patrystycznej* [Anthology of Patristic Literature], Vol. 1. Warsaw: PAX, 1975.

Myszor, Wincenty. "Wstęp" [Introduction] to *Teksty z Nag-Hammadi* [Texts from Nag-Hammadi]. Warsaw: Akademia Teologii Katolickiej, 1979.

Nock, Arthur Darby. *Conversion: The Old and the New in Religion from Alexander the Great to Augustine of Hippo.* Baltimore: Johns Hopkins University Press, 1998.

Origen. *Contra Celsum.* Translated by Henry Chadwick. Cambridge: Cambridge University Press, 1980.

Osborn, Eric. *The Beginning of Christian Philosophy.* Cambridge: Cambridge University Press, 1981.

————. *The Emergence of Christian Theology.* Cambridge: Cambridge University Press, 1993.

————. *Irenaeus of Lyons.* Cambridge: Cambridge University Press, 2001.

————. *Justin Martyr.* Tübingen: Mohr, 1973.

———. *The Philosophy of Clement of Alexandria.* Cambridge: Cambridge University Press, 1957.

———. *Tertullian: First Theologian of the West.* Cambridge: Cambridge University Press, 1997.

Pelikan, Jaroslav. *Christianity and Classical Culture: The Metamorphosis of Natural Theology in the Christian Encounter with Hellenism.* New Haven: Yale University Press, 1993.

———. *The Emergence of the Catholic Tradition.* Chicago: University of Chicago Press, 1975.

Philo of Alexandria. *On the Creation of the Cosmos according to Moses.* Translated by David T. Runia. Leiden: Brill, 2001.

Pindar. *Roman Lives.* Translated by Robin Waterfield. Oxford: Oxford University Press, 1992.

Plato. *Phaedo.* Translated by David Gallop. Oxford: Oxford University Press, 2009.

Plutarch. *Roman Lives.* Translated by Robin Waterfield. Oxford: Oxford University Press, 1999.

Quispel, Gilles. *Gnostica, Judaica, and Catholica: Collected Essays of Gilles Quispel.* Leiden: Brill, 2008.

Rankin, David. *Tertulian and the Church.* Cambridge: Cambridge University Press, 1995.

Schaff, Philip, ed. *Ante-Nicene Fathers.* New York: Christian Literature Company, 1885.

———. *Nicene and Post-Nicene Fathers.* New York: Christian Literature Company, 1900.

Skarsaune, Oskar. *The Proof from Prophecy: A Study in Justin Martyr's Proof-Text Tradition: Text-Type, Provenance, Theological Profile.* Leiden: Brill, 1987.

Simon, Marcel. *Cywilizacja wczesnego chrześcijaństwa* [Early Christian Civilization]. Translated by Eligia Bąkowska. Warsaw: PIW, 1981.

Stępień, Tomasz. "Ojcowie Kościoła i demon Sokratesa" [Fathers of the Church and the Daimonion of Socrates]. In *Teologia Polityczna* [Political Theology] 2. (2004–5) 242–51.

Shestov, Lev. *Athens and Jerusalem.* Translated by Bernard Martin. Athens, OH: Ohio University Press, 1966.

Wilken, Robert L. *The Christians as the Roman Saw Them.* New Haven: Yale University Press, 1984.

Zieliński, Jacek. *Jerozolimy, Ateny, Aleksandria* [Jerusalem, Athens, Alexandria]. Wroclaw: Wroclaw University Publishers, 2000.

Index